TALES OF INNOCENCE AND EXPERIENCE

An Exploration

Eva Figes

BLOOMSBURY

Published by Bloomsbury, New York and London
Distributed to the trade by Holtzbrinck Publishers

ISBN 1-58234-259-8

First U.S. Edition 2003

1 3 5 7 9 10 8 6 4 2

Typeset by Hewer Text Ltd, Edinburgh
Printed in Great Britain by Clays Limited, St Ives plc

TALES OF INNOCENCE
AND EXPERIENCE

Fiction

Equinox
Winter Journey
Konek Landing
B
Days
Nelly's Version
Waking
Light
The Seven Ages
Ghosts
The Tree of Knowledge
The Tenancy
The Knot

Non-Fiction

Patriarchal Attitudes
Tragedy and Social Evolution
Little Eden
Sex and Subterfuge

For
Alice and Lydia,
Eleanor and Grace

ONE

I

What was the best Christmas present you ever had?

Her head is on my lap, legs stretched out on the sofa. Holding up her right arm to admire the bracelet of plastic daisies on her wrist, the fingers of her left hand fiddling with it. She is replete, exhausted. Every package has been opened, every mystery has revealed its secret. The waste-paper basket is full of shiny paper and bits of ribbon. The air of the living room is slightly stuffy with odours of alcohol and food, pine branches and burnt-out candles.

I spent the night here to share the magic her birth has rekindled, arriving just as dusk was falling and every window in the street glowed with lamplight or winking Christmas tree lights left on in a dark bay window. I was weighed down with packages, but the bulkiest was of course for her, which she guessed as soon as she ran to the front door in a frenzy of excitement. Her little body was electric, eyes shining, face flushed. She could not keep still. Tonight the universe was benign, and I was happy. A legend had been reborn, for a moment, and tawdry tinsel glittered with distant starlight.

Food and drink were put out for Santa, a carrot for the reindeer, and she worried that everything was just so, hovering near the hearth. If only, if only it would snow, she sighed, peering into the dark. It still might, I told her, ignoring the weather forecast. Anything might happen tonight. Especially if you hurry up and go to sleep. From her upstairs window I could see a cloudless sky and a sickle moon beyond leafless trees.

Did you have snow when you were a child?

Oh yes, I said, very deep. Always. And Christmas trees as far as the eye could see. Miles of them.

She wriggled under the duvet and let out a wistful sound. I'm going to shut my eyes and imagine snowflakes falling, then perhaps it will happen.

Good idea. The sooner you get to sleep, the sooner Father Christmas will come.

He's been! I heard her yell shortly after five in the morning.

Bleary-eyed, we sat round the miracle child in her pink pyjamas and watched her small fingers unwrap the miniature presents stuffed into the gigantic stocking, almost, if not quite bottomless. Each colourful package reveals its magic, evokes astonishment, cries of delight. Sipping a first cup of tea, we sit round in dressing gowns, watching, an echoing chorus. Unto us a child is born. We are all tired, but happy.

But that was hours ago, long before daylight reduced the coloured intensity of the lights on the tree. Now the tantalizing packages lying under it have been revealed for what they are, expensive things bought from shops by grown-ups. No wish left unfulfilled, plus a superfluity

4

beyond imagining. Now she is tired, beyond satiety. The plastic bracelet she is admiring on her thin little arm was found in a cracker at lunch.

The pram you bought me is my best present.

She tilts her head back to smile at me, eyes looking into my eyes.

Good, I say, stroking her hair, which is soft and blonde, but will go darker.

I had gone all over town looking for it, after she had seen a child pushing a pram in the park and asked if I would buy her one. But making her happy is still easy. If she had asked for the moon I would have tried to get it.

She thinks all this will go on for ever. The room, the tree, the winking lights. Every December. Which is why she is asking about my childhood.

What was the best present you ever had?

2

It was, I say, a wonderful doll's house.

I am conscious of choosing my words carefully. I always do when I tell her about the distant past. She smiles, eyes bright, as if it had only just happened.

My granny bought it for me.

The link in the chain is made. I want it, she does too. Idly she strokes the back of my hand, fascinated by its protruding veins. She follows them with her forefinger every time I hold her, bewitched by their untold story. But now she is waiting for the story of the doll's house to continue.

It was just like our house, only tiny. All the chairs, the dining table, sideboard. Even the cups and saucers and the cutlery. And the lamps really lit up, and real water came out of the taps in the bathroom.

I go on stroking her silky hair. I do not tell her about the packing crates in the empty dining room, how I too was told I could only put in the bits of furniture, not the house. Like our rooms, it would stay behind, empty. How, for years after, I would push the tiny replicas into position, imagining the lost walls. And did so too with the furniture, too large for new rooms they were never meant to occupy.

3

Tonight she is very sleepy, and I want the bedtime story to be soothing. No sudden shocks, nothing scary. What matters is the sound of my voice, reassuring as a lullaby. The picture book on my lap is *Little Red Riding Hood*, but I speak from memory. I am this child, her story is familiar as my own, seems to be my own. I know each tree, every sunlit clearing, the echo of birdsong high in the canopy, beyond it glimpses of blue sky. I tell her about finding pine cones, and soft patches of dark green moss, and how much the little girl and her grandmother loved each other. How it was the old lady who had made her the red velvet cap which the child always wore, not only because she liked it so much, but because her grandmother had made it for her, and that made it even more special.

She lay very still, watching my face. Eyes wide and unblinking, thumb in her mouth.

I said how she loved walking in the woods, because they were beautiful, and at the end of her walk would be her grandmother's little house, which was the nicest and safest place she knew, quiet and comforting and always the same. And the old lady was always the same too, ready to talk and listen and give her homebaked gingerbread when she was hungry.

I look down at her flushed face on the pillow and see from the dark eyes and enlarged pupils that she has entered another world. My own is receding. Just a glimmer of yellow light between the looming shadows of trees.

I lower my voice to a whisper, stroking her head. Although she had heard of the big bad wolf, I murmur, she did not believe in him, since he was only a fairy tale, and the path through the wood was both familiar and a journey of magical surprises, whether it was a cobweb sparkling with morning dew or the bushy tail of a red squirrel glimpsed for a moment.

I feel her small warm body turn and draw closer, eyes closing.

Moving cautiously, I get up, bend over to kiss her forehead, breathe in her sweet odour, and tiptoe out of the room.

4

A dull, overcast day. The new year is born old, as usual. Grey and shop-soiled and dreary. The idea of a new beginning, resolutions great or small, no longer even enters my head. January represents continuity: my new diary may have a different cover but inside the weekly format is indistinguishable from the old. The entries may vary slightly, but not significantly.

The tree, its few needles brown and dry, lies on its side by the area railing, drab and skeletal. A strand of silver left in its naked crest, a memento of lost glory.

The child, however, is covered in newness. A bright new hat with matching scarf, new boots, and furry mitts with cats' faces on the back, complete with ears and whiskers. We are going to take a new doll, given the name of Daisy, for her first outing to the park in the brand-new pram. It is a major undertaking, and I need to lend a hand with steps, kerbs and crossings. She peers under the hood to tell the doll that she is going to the park, but Daisy is lying with her eyes shut.

In a stage whisper I am told that the doll is asleep.

We go through the gates of the park, where solitary men, muffled up against the cold, are walking their dogs. Brown earth in the empty flowerbeds, leafless trees.

I wish it would snow, she says, surveying the chilly scene.

It might, I tell her, pointing to the low-lying clouds above us.

How do you know?

Well, the clouds look right for it. When they look like dirty old pillows, there is an old woman up there who shakes out her bedding, and out come, not feathers, but flakes of snow.

Really?

There is a slightly doubtful expression as she looks me in the eye.

What's her name?

Mother Holle.

That's a funny name.

She laughs, then tilts her head back to look up at the sky.

Come on, Mother Holle, she shouts, can you hear me? We want some snow.

We get up from the bench where we have been sitting for a moment and head for the playground. I have to take charge of the pram as she runs on ahead.

She sits down on a vacant swing and I begin to push.

Higher! she shrieks.

A snow crystal lands on my sleeve, melts. Then another. She tilts her head back in the swing and sees snowflakes coming down towards her. Sticks her tongue out. When she gets off they are caught in her eyelashes, in her woolly hat and scarf.

What did you say her name was?
Who?
The lady who shakes down the snow.
Mother Holle.
Is she married to Father Christmas?
I don't think so, no.
I never knew about her before. I'm going to ask her again.
She begins to skip with excitement.
Then I can make a snowman. And go sledging. But I haven't got a sledge. Next year, will you buy me a sledge?
Maybe.
The snow is melting as fast as it falls.

I hear children's voices ringing in the clear sharp air, small dark figures sliding down the slope opposite. Everything else is bright white, other than a few leafless branches sticking out of the snow. I am standing at the top of the opposite slope, excitedly chattering in a high-pitched voice. Where is this magic winter playground to which my grandparents have brought me, each one holding me by a hand? A miniature oasis framed in mist. My grandfather sits on the sledge and puts me between his outstretched legs and we slide down very slowly, his feet braking our cautious descent, which comes to a stop far too quickly, by an outcrop of rock under a leafless sapling, whilst my grandmother, on the gravel footpath above us, applauds.

Where is it now, where was it?

Standing in the playground, she tilts her head back, mouth wide open, tongue sticking out.

It tastes cold, she says.

She holds her gloved hands outstretched to catch the falling flakes, and together we look closely at them before they turn to water.

Each snow crystal, I tell her, is different from every other, so no two snowflakes are the same. Every one has its own pattern.

She stares long and hard at her warmly protected palm with its dark wet patch.

Not when they've melted, she says sadly.

5

Snow falling on Christmas Eve is a child's notion of the miraculous, particularly on an island with a mild climate where rain or drizzle is far more likely. Even in parts of the world where snow never falls the image of peaceful villages sleeping under a white blanket sent from heaven is cherished as part of the Christmas legend. It is in fact the Christmas legend, replacing the star in the East over a desert landscape as a portent of heavenly grace, of a better future.

Why is this so? Snow is purity, a dream of innocence. The child can play with it, whilst the rest of us see in the winter landscape the mirage of a clean sheet, a new beginning, pristine fields unmarked by human footfalls, old journeys, mistaken enterprises. So, on Christmas morning, the world should be newly born, and if every roof, every untrodden street, every bare branch and flowerless back yard is suddenly shrouded in virgin beauty the sharp cold of it stops us short, breathless.

If only I did not know that nothing stays frozen in the moment. How dark pockmarks will appear within hours, footprints turn to dirty mush, the grit lorry will scatter its load so human traffic can carry on as usual.

And then the Christmas tree. Not an eastern palm,

heavy with fruit. Not even a British oak, or any broadleaf emblem of death and renewal. A fir-tree, prickly, with only an inedible harvest, used to cold weather, to sandy unpromising soil, symbol of darkness at the heart of the forest. Cover it with sweetmeats, light the candles, garnish it with baubles, place a toy angel or a holy star on its spiky tip, but do not forget where it came from, what it represents.

The forest is dark, black, comes from the earth. Snow might fall on it, heavenly, pure, but the forest endures, hides its secrets. It is always there, at the edge of things. Children go into it, and do not emerge. Only in fairy tales do they survive, and then only after terrible things have happened to them. So garland the fir-tree, switch on the lights, and sing. Let the bells ring out to warn off the hungry wolf, and promise the children their heart's desire.

6

Nevertheless, the sharp odour of pine forest triggers memory, so the heart aches. It was only dangerous after nightfall, I knew that, when I was safely tucked up in bed and could listen with impunity to the story of Hänsel and Gretel abandoned in the thick of it, or how Snow-White ran from the killer's knife, the wolf prowling with hungry eyes in the dark. In daylight, adult members of the family safely within earshot, it was a pleasure zone of light and shade, full of unending surprises, mushrooms and pine cones or an oozing bark to signify that a stag had been here, rubbing its antlers. I could run ahead, peering and prying, just as long as I could hear their voices through the trees, catch a glimpse of their outlines. It was children on their own who were in peril, I knew that, which was why, seeing a photograph of myself standing solitary surrounded by forest, I experienced a moment of panic. It had to be explained to me that of course I was not alone, my father and mother had been on the far side of the camera.

7

I enter into her world. Or rather, I watch, as I would an iridescent bubble, or a crimson poppy trembling on its stalk. I am breathless with its fragility, anxious to protect it from harm.

The weather is reasonably good, and I am taking her to the zoo. A trip to the zoo is like leafing through a child's alphabet book, from aardvark to zebra. Here they all are, the wonders of creation, just as they once marched out of the ark which Noah built. In all their particularity, large and small, grey and yellow, striped and spotted. Safely behind bars or on the other side of a deep moat, with keepers who know just what to do with them. The elephant lifts an enormous leg or waves his trunk in the air. Penguins dive into the blue pool for fish. The tiger leans harmlessly against a panel of unbreakable glass whilst she presses her palms on its smooth surface, studying its thick pelt close to. Chimpanzees shriek and show off their circus acrobatics, responsive to high-pitched children's laughter and pointing fingers on the far side of the wire.

Her short legs tire easily, so I sit her down with an ice cream. By this time we have seen most of the very obvious attractions, the legendary forms of creation. The rare panda, looking like a huge cuddly toy, rubbery camels with floppy humps, elongated giraffes with flirty eyelashes and only a tentative relationship with the ground beneath their delicate hooves. Now she wants a drink. I think she also needs to go to the lavatory. She asks if I will buy her something in the shop, and if she can queue up for a ride on the pony. On our way to the shop she sees the playground and wants to swing on the bars, get on the seesaw, ride the roundabout. I point out that we could do all this at home, and try to get her away. It seems that small children are not so different from their cousins, the baby chimps, when it comes to doing what comes naturally. The playground is crowded. After endless hesitation and several changes of mind we emerge from the shop with a plastic elephant.

On our way to the lavatory we find ourselves passing the wolf enclosure. It is off the beaten track, an unpretentious wire enclosure full of ordinary shrubs and small trees. It looks like a forgotten wasteland, waiting for the developers to move in. I have heard there is a plan to move them elsewhere, but for now the creatures, looking little different from the Alsatian dogs so often paraded in the local park by young men with shaven heads and conspicuous tattoos, still slink through the undergrowth. I read somewhere that people living nearby hear them howl in the night, but now they are almost eerily quiet.

After tea we settle down on the sofa to read a story. She is very tired and snuggles against me, looking at the bright, simplified pictures. The wolf, wearing her grandmother's frilly nightcap, looks comical, a wolf in human clothing. The child is duly deceived.

She shouldn't talk to strangers, had been her only comment so far, when Red Riding Hood met the wolf on her walk through the wood, and told him where she was going. My mummy says not to.

Quite right, I remark, breaking off from my reading.

If she hadn't told him where she was going her granny would have been all right.

Maybe. But –

Did her mummy not tell her about the wolf?

No, she didn't. My tone is apologetic. Perhaps she did not know about him. Or she didn't want to frighten her little girl.

I glanced down at her thoughtful face, and realized she was considering the possibility that parents did not always tell their children the whole truth. Hurriedly I returned to the printed text, using my story voice. Rather to my surprise she accepted the emergence of Red Riding Hood and her grandmother from the wolf's stomach, not so much as a toothmark on either of them, without question. And when the wolf collapsed and died because his belly was full of heavy stones she laughed heartily. She found his death unambiguously comic, and began to mimic the situation by staggering round the room, holding her belly and pulling faces.

8

I do not know why her birth struck such terror into me. I felt joy, of course, but I had not expected this emotion. I thought at first it was fear. It had been so long since I gave birth to a child of my own, and I was no longer used to handling such fragility, the eggshell skull, the neck unable to hold its weight. For months I found myself wrestling with conflicting emotions: loving tenderness, and a fear of what I might do to her. Perhaps it was not merely anxiety concerning my own ineptitude, the added responsibility of minding a child who was not my own, but my daughter's first-born. A friend of mine who had become a grand-mother at about the same time and who also found herself subject to the same emotions felt it had to do with power, and over the next few weeks I reluctantly came to the conclusion that she was probably right. As ageing women with children who have long since flown the nest, minding the newborn baby gives us a potency, restores a potency lost years ago. Harming the helpless infant in our care, whether by accident or design, could hurt as nothing else could do. The despised old crone of the fairy tale doing her worst, wreaking vengeance on the young, on the innocent. The Medea lurking in every one of us.

We assign Medea to the realms of myth, but it was

Euripides who had her kill her children in order to hurt a faithless husband she could touch in no other way. Freud did not identify a Medea complex, nor did his followers, but I suspect that every mother who has been abandoned by a faithless husband knows about the wild demon lurking deep inside, and fears losing control of it. I think it is the conscientious, loving mother who fears her most, the woman who would never strike a child in anger, or do less than her utmost to make it secure and happy, whose children mean more to her than life itself. It is because she is this way that, at certain times, she fears loss of control, that the demon will escape from the stoppered bottle, the evil whirlwind will strike, and ruin her life utterly. I have felt her, Medea, prickling under my skin long ago.

And then there is fragility itself, what it does to us, how it affects us. I used to have a fantasy, that I would enter the glass and china section of a department store and smash everything on display, that insanity would seize hold of me and I would do wilful damage, simply because it was a possibility.

A newborn baby is like that, provoking dread. Of a moment's inattention, or worse.

Luckily, my angst quickly subsided. With every passing day, as I grew to know her, as she grew to recognize me, as the bond between us, my role in her life strengthened with her body. Out of practice perhaps, but I knew I could trust myself to mind her, keep her safe, if anyone could. That their trust in me was not misplaced.

I had a role. I was the granny, the wise old woman, who made her grandchild a pretty red cap. Not the despised old crone, the evil witch who ate children for supper.

9

Absolute innocence is absolute trust, which is so horrifying. A toddler holding the hand of his killer and walking off to his death, caught on a security camera, freezes the blood. That is why the story of Hänsel and Gretel is a fairy tale. We assume that Hänsel is a survivor, the boy old enough to know how evil the world is, who uses his wits to escape capture, knowing that resettlement is a journey to certain death.

Yes, Hänsel is a survivor. He listens at doors, plans ahead whilst his little sister weeps, trusts nobody but himself, is inventive and cunning, ruthless in a tight spot. Born into poverty and hardship, he has long since left childhood behind, crossed the borderline between innocence and harsh experience. The story of Hänsel and Gretel is, like so many tales handed down by tradition, a tale of bravery and initiative against improbable odds in a natural environment where everything except their own wits is stacked against them. The forest is dark, the witch is evil, poor people, far from cherishing their children, want to get rid of them.

Childhood is a modern invention. We sanitize the old stories, as we do history. I sit on the sofa with the picture book open on my lap, whilst she snuggles warmly into my side. It is part of the story-time ritual that I put my right arm round her, giving comfort and security, whilst I turn the pages with my left hand. Daylight beyond the window, slanting across the page. I stop to point out incidental details in the coloured illustrations, an owl perched on a branch, the roof of the gingerbread house, which looks deliciously edible. I reiterate, as I have done on previous occasions, that witches do not exist in real life, only in stories.

How far does landscape shape the human psyche? What happens to a nation where myth and territory dangerously converge? The child cosying up to me on the sofa has never walked through more than half a dozen trees, usually in the local park. The country into which she was born is a place of small open fields with sheltering hedges, the odd copse, an occasional stream. It is a land which has buried its past, no longer has secrets.

But I was born in a country where immense forest lay at the edge of everything, fringing the city, lurking on the verge of consciousness where sense and civilized living gave way to a dark worship of trees and their mystery. It began where the tramcar reached its terminus, and stretched I knew not where. Only stretches of water held it back, providing a breathing space, freedom and a reflection of sky, but trees came right to the water's edge. We walked in its shadowed spaces, finding traces of deer and wild boar, but did not control it.

The forest is a place of retreat, escape, of romantic longing. But it is also dark and dangerous, a place where civilized behaviour gives way to evil forces, to murder and mayhem, secret and unseen. Shots ring out in the silence, and it is not the wounded stag who falls. Children go into the forest, and do not come out. Older people, too, vanish into its depths and are not seen again. Years later unmarked graves are found, hidden in undergrowth. The forest keeps its secrets under last year's leaves.

The beauty that I saw with my child's eyes has lost its innocent purity. I see shadows, not light. Evil has come out of the story books and is now history. The child happily exploring every bush and pathway knew nothing of past, present and future, only the shining hour.

She was born in the spring, as I was too. It seems a propitious season for such an event. Birds, busily nest-building, chirp in the branches of trees, just breaking into palest green. The tentative snowdrop has long since opened in winter earth, as did the crocus with its first hint of colour, and now we are in the thick of it, brash daffodils trumpeting their presence in every street and garden, imported tulips sold in every possible hue, streaked, parrot, or simply pink.

The air is milder, the sky, if changeable, is promising. It lengthens our day, stays light for longer before withdrawing.

April is the cruellest month, growls the poet, but for once I refuse to let age and experience contaminate my sense of rebirth. This spring marks a true beginning, not merely the weary recycling of a tired planet.

For days my daughter looks bruised and battered by the experience, dark shadows under her eyes, haunted by a new expression which deepens their colour. She knows what she did not know before, that she is merely a link in the chain, to be used and discarded. The myth of the sacred individual has been shattered, discarded. Women lose their innocence, not with the loss of virginity, but with childbirth.

This is a truth I learnt when she was born, and I was younger than she is now, and I had only just begun to piece together my shattered ego after upheaval and catastrophe. And then the most ancient law of nature took hold of my body and used it, ruthlessly. Now my pallid, storm-tossed daughter looks at me from the bed, the pillows propping her up, and our eyes meet in a new understanding, bridging the gap of time. It is hard for her in a different way, not a child of war but a child of peace, indulged, unthreatened, playtime extended indefinitely, even sex a toy. Now the shock of the oldest law, spoken by God to the first woman, is in her eyes. There is no escape. I think of the young virgins, hardly more than children, sacrificed on the altar of matrimony. I think of my own girlhood and the terror and taboo which were part of growing up. And the complicity of older women in pretending the agony was less than I might think. And I, who had not thought, lulled by the latest medical myth of painless birth. Unable to imagine the unimaginable, putting my faith in progressive science. Justifiably, of course. Nevertheless, the old law has not been repealed, and the purpose of birth is also the purpose of death.

12

Nevertheless, a new beginning and the coming of spring, what more could a woman of my age, with nothing else to hope for, want? I come bringing gifts, spring flowers and a portion of homemade chicken soup, and the first genuine gift of many years is put into my arms, skin still red raw, eyes unfocused and blinking in light from the window. Her helpless vulnerability, my sudden sense of inadequacy, takes my breath away. Only for a moment. I have forgotten what it was like, those early days. Although she looks like a skinned rabbit, utterly exposed, she is also perfection, with tiny hands and feet and the correct number of fingers and toes and adorable nails. The skin will grow white, her eyes the colour of deep water will soon learn to focus, to recognize and smile. Her fingers curl round mine even now, in the required manner.

I am a grandmother. Through no effort of my own, merely length of life, I have been given this role. All I need to do is be there for her, enter into her world. I know this. The ghost of my lost grandmother speaks to me now. I feel her looking over my shoulder. She taught me how easy it is, just so long as you go on living. The will to survive is required.

13

With the birth of a child comes the opportunity to re-enter the kingdom of heaven. It will not last long, but for a brief period it is possible to re-experience the world made new, in all its freshness. What else, after all, is the Garden of Eden, except the glory of the world seen through the eyes of innocence?

I recollect how it was, the particularity of every leaf, each blade of grass with the dew still damp, sun just rising over neighbouring rooftops, glinting in the branches of trees, and I watching a slow insect crawling into the heart of a half-open rose, or carefully examining grains of sand, finding out each was a jewel of hidden colour and shape, unique and precious. Losing it, too suddenly, not gradually as each and every one of us must lose it, as the dew dries in the light of common day, but violently, in a winter which seemed to have no end, so that the colours glow more brightly at the far end of a long dark tunnel, always visible and always out of reach.

I get weary, we all do, with the light of common day. I marvel for a moment, staring at a tree glistening with rainbow drops after a sudden shower, and get on with the routine. I have been taught in school about the composition of light. When my schooling had only just begun my mother still used prismatic knife rests, a foreign custom, and at every meal I would put them to my eyes to see the dismal little dining room, part of our new home, transformed by myriad rainbows on every chair, every angle. I would laugh, my brother would also laugh, viewing each other and the room whilst my mother silently served up food, but by then I knew it was only an optical illusion. Outside the window, when I began to eat my mashed potato, was a treeless asphalt yard and a row of lock-up garages.

But now a child is born, and with it a chance to sneak back into the garden of innocence, even if it is only make-believe, an illusion.

A vicarious experience for us, but not for her. And so we watch intently as her eyes follow the movements of a bird, of a toy balloon, as her hand goes out to a shining bauble on the Christmas tree or the flame on the solitary candle of her first birthday cake. Eagerly we blow bubbles, dandelion clocks, ring tinkling bells, make toy rabbits squeak and hop. Not content to create a safe environment for her to play in, we create the illusion of a harmless universe, the nursery as Eden. The room is full of cuddly bears and toothless tigers, lion and lamb walk side by side on the wallpaper frieze, bluebirds dip and dive on the end of pieces of string. The pages of the alphabet book begin with an unbitten apple, round, flawless.

I find myself drawn to the windows of toyshops, particularly if they specialize in old-fashioned toys, Victorian dolls, wooden Noah's arks, clowns in baggy satin, reproduction doll's houses with Georgian façades, a graceful rocking horse going nowhere, steam engines, toys for adults with deep pockets and deeper memories. Not only personal memories, but memory as myth, the idyll of the story book, the invention of childhood itself, girls with long hair, boys in sailor suits, rolling hoops in the park, looking for fairies at the bottom of the garden, finding elves in the attic.

But it is in my own attic that I find my daughter's first baby toy, a woolly lamb with a bell round its neck. The white wool is grey, the blue of the ribbon holding the bell has faded. Why did I, why did she choose not to throw it away? It was never lost, to tell the truth, for years it just lay amongst the clutter, gathering dust. I could not throw it away. Unwilling to take it with her when she left, she could not, it seems, throw it into the dustbin either.

I give it a good scrub with a nailbrush and it emerges hygienic, historic too. On my next visit I give it to my grown-up child who, without a word, puts it in the cot, near to her sleeping child's head.

14

Once upon a time, I hear my voice say, reading from the page, and the words seem to come from a great distance, in the middle of winter, and I see the landscape glistening in moonlight, once upon a time I begin, the beginning of all beginnings, when the flakes of snow were falling like feathers from the sky, and I knew Mother Holle was shaking her pillows up in the sky and the thick grey clouds were feather bedding, a Queen sat at her window sewing, and the frame of the window was made of black ebony.

What's ebony?

Her blonde head is resting against me, so she can see the pictures. Fair hair, like her father.

I tell her. It is black, black as black can be. I see it now, the dark frame, white snow sparkling. Absolutes. I see black against white, a window which always seemed mysterious.

And whilst she was sewing and looking out of the window at the snow, she pricked her finger with the needle, and three drops of blood fell upon the snow.

Ouch! she looks up at me and laughs.

I laugh back. Silly Queen, she wasn't paying attention, was she? Needles are sharp.

And scissors.

Quite right.

I resume my story-telling voice.

And the red looked pretty upon the white snow, and she thought to herself: Would that I had a child as white as snow, as red as blood, and as black as the wood of the window frame.

I found it strange even then, my mother's voice evoking a world of dark wood, a magic place where blood looks pretty on snow. I found it a strange wish, fateful, for an unborn child. Everyone knew it was best to have blonde hair and blue eyes. I knew things would go badly for Snow-White.

Your golden hair Margarete, your ashen hair Shulamith

I had decided, at the age of five, to have blue eyes when I grew up. As for my hair, it was middling, a mousy colour. It rendered me invisible in the streets. My brother was the darling of strangers, his hair so fair, angelic. I stood by, silent, as he got patted on the head. The policeman on the corner took a boiled sweet out of his top pocket and gave it to him. I got nothing.

I continue with the sad tale of Snow-White, conceived in midwinter, with her black hair and unearthly skin, her mother duly dying as the child was born.

Alarm bells ring in my head even as I read out the words. Hastily I explain that in the olden days, long, long ago, women did occasionally die when they had a baby, but not now, definitely not. My daughter is expecting her second child, and her first-born is beginning to show quite sufficient signs of childish insecurity as it is, without worrying about losing her mother entirely.

She puts her thumb in her mouth.

The new Queen, her stepmother, was very proud and haughty, and could not bear that anyone should surpass her in beauty.

She takes her thumb out of her mouth to ask: What colour was her hair?

Do you know, that's a very good question. The story doesn't say.

I read on to the bit where the Queen consults the magic mirror. Who in the land is the fairest one of all?

So she's got fair hair.

Possibly.

But then how can Snow-White be the fairest, when her hair is black?

My eye on the page, I hastily explain that in olden days, long ago and far away, the word fair also meant beautiful. The little girl with her snowy skin —

My friend Gemma has black hair *and* black skin, she interjects.

The doorbell rings. Her mother has come to collect her, putting an end to story-telling. I shut the book, telling her that this story happened long ago and far away, where nobody had ever seen someone like her friend Gemma.

This didn't happen in England then?

No.

In a country of dark forests, where crimes go unwitnessed. In a forest full of secrets, shadows, unending vistas which lead nowhere, where a child will feel lost if its parents hide behind a tree, if only for a moment, heart-stopping seconds when a bird calls mockingly in the echoing silence and a twig cracks too loudly, sharply, somewhere, and I can hear my own breath going in and out, standing stock-still, rooted to the spot, if I move my foot the sound is scary, sudden and unexpected in the stillness, and the forest too is holding its breath, until I do move forward, this way or that, regardless, for every direction is the same direction, and I am lost, hopelessly.

Snow-White, I tell my grandchild, was only seven years old when her beauty caught the eye of the magic mirror. The girl was growing up, and though she was still only a child by our reckoning the wicked Queen knew it was time to be rid of her. Today I am sticking to the text, and she is quietly attentive. So she was just seven years old when her stepmother told the huntsman to take her rival into the forest and butcher her. The huntsman did as he was told, for he was in the habit of obeying orders, and even the instruction to bring back the child's lung and liver as proof of her death did not make him unduly squeamish. Killing warm-blooded living creatures was his job. So he had already pulled out his knife and was about to carry out his orders when Snow-White unexpectedly began to plead with him, promising to vanish into the forest, and never go back home. If only he would spare her. And the child was so beautiful that the huntsman took pity on her. After all he was just an ordinary man, who usually liked children, dandled them on his knee and knew how to carve little wooden toys with his sharp knife. No doubt he had a family of his own, whom he loved and petted at the end of a hard day's work.

So the huntsman told her to run away, into the forest, fully aware that the little girl did not stand a chance, since the wild beasts would quickly devour her. But it was a great weight off his mind, knowing he did not have to kill her himself. There were times when he did not like his job, and this was one of them. He could simply leave the girl to be torn limb from limb by wolves or bears and fob off his despotic mistress with the lungs and liver of a young boar which happened to be running by just then. The deception worked, and the Queen ate them, duly cooked and salted, with relish, convinced that she was devouring her step-child.

As for the dwarfs, they told the terrified child that she could stay with them only provided she did the cooking, kept the house clean, knitted and sewed. Their supper had to be ready for them when they got back from the mine at night. Attempted murder and cannibalism followed by child labour, hard and unrelenting: tough going for a seven-year-old. They might be charmed by her beauty, but dwarfs who mine for copper and gold in the earth are legendary for their hard-headed greed.

It is a wonder that the child survived, an accident really. The wicked Queen was unrelenting in her pursuit of the young girl, and the poisoned apple was her fourth attempt to get rid of her. If the prince's servitors had not stumbled over a tree stump whilst carrying the glass coffin, dislodging the piece of apple stuck in her throat, Snow-White would have stayed frozen for ever, an object of display, of mourning and regret.

Woods are an echo chamber, a labyrinth of dreams, forgotten sounds and smells which trigger memory. Small twigs snap under my foot. I am here, in my adopted country. I am far off, in a lost homeland. Only trees, cutting out every horizon, make me think that time past and time future are both perhaps here, in time present. That nothing is ever quite lost. I am old. I am still very, very young. I wonder at the timelessness of nature's creation, and allow myself to forget, for this moment outside time, its utter desecration by the human race. Unlike the trees, I do not have roots, walking here reminds me of it. Or perhaps, on the contrary, I am instantly at home anywhere which offers a canopy of branches high overhead, where odorous pine needles lie underfoot and colonnades of tall trunks open only on to partial vistas and uncertain paths.

The hollow call of the cuckoo, mocking, woody, is the same in any language. I am here it says, look for me, find me. We are here, it says, your ghosts, lurking amongst the trees, just out of sight. Footsteps on dead leaves, a voice half heard, a figure glimpsed for a moment. Find us, find us.

17

She comes to me on a regular basis, and otherness mingles with familiarity. She knows where the biscuits, quite different from those at home, are to be found, and is avid for them. The toy drawer, with games she does not play in her own house, is conveniently at floor level, and she always wants to play shop. I have a grand piano, not an upright, and here she can play house, or hide when a parent arrives to take her home. She asks to go up and play in the attic, simply because it exists, cold, dusty, unused. She peers at the various objects on my dressing table, looks at herself afresh in the mirror, tries out my shoes, slipping and sliding in their vastness.

All this is precious to her, familiar but not. An otherness which is also home. Dead people peer out of photographs, from an epoch she finds mysterious and unfathomable. Looking at a family group which includes my father in a boy's sailor suit, she asks if I am also in the picture. She opens my old metronome, listening to the ticktock of time, adagio, presto. She always steps on my bathroom scales, curious about her own growth. As for staying the night, this is so exciting that she insists on having her bath far too early, gets into bed, and then comes down every five minutes, quite unable to sleep.

Colours, smells, tastes. The texture of things, and the way light falls across the room. She is building up memories, I know this, but she does not. Assembling a knowledge of place, the particularity of this, also her territory. And together, week by week, we create our own rituals, dutiful, playful, which exist only here, belong to the two of us. I am here for her, only for her, and she knows it. Which is why she is content, quick to obey, wash her hands or tidy up, it is all part of the game we play together, the rewards, surprises, the ability to say what is on her mind, troubling her. This is a conflict-free zone, reassuring, comforting. My wisdom may be bogus, but she believes in it, because I am old, beyond the fray, because I have magic in my fingertips when she hurts herself. I cast a spell and blow the pain away.

Years from now, she will remember, the walls, the smell of basil on the windowsill, the way light fell from the high windows, rooftops and a network of old trees, the telephone in the corner of the hall with its dark green wallpaper. She will take them down, one at a time, the wooden animals from Africa, and line them up as she used to do, under the piano. Some time in the future, unable to sleep, she will shut her eyes in the dark and put back the walls, the bookshelves, the pot of basil on the windowsill, every last stick of furniture, for the comfort of finding a lost childhood, of once again walking from room to room, recovering what time has destroyed, turning the clock back, sick with longing for someone who will always blow the pain away, and keep her safe.

I know how it is. I watch her, peering over edges, reaching things she has so far only yearned to touch, pulling herself up to look out of the window, climbing on to a stool to open the biscuit tin, turning door knobs and taps more easily, seeing how the trees have begun to change colour, how far the needle on the bathroom scales will swing on this occasion.

I know how it is, and how it will be. I remember the dimly lit bathroom, how I would open the door on every visit just to sniff it, the heavy scent of my grandmother's perfume. I still do, in the night.

Grandmother, what big eyes you have.

She is sitting astride my lap, smiling. Eyes bright with expectancy.

All the better to see you with.

My voice is growly. I peer at her with mock ferocity from under my eyebrows.

Grandmother, what a big nose you have.

Her grin is gleeful.

All the better to sniff you with.

I begin to snuffle round her neck and chin, over the surface of her wriggling, giggling body, holding her tight by her arms so she does not slip to the floor and hurt herself.

Grandmother, what a big mouth you have.

My words merge into mock growls as I pretend to gobble her up, smelling the sweetness of her, the soft skin between ear and shoulder, there where it is most pleasurable to bite and be bitten. The breath goes out of her with laughter. Her cheeks are bright pink.

Again! she clamours, breathless.

The journey of memory is not a regular trajectory from now to then, an exercise in perspective, everything getting smaller and dimmer as the unbending road stretches to the horizon. No. At some point in time it begins to turn back on itself, so yesterday and last year are wreathed in an indeterminate fog, but childhood reasserts itself. Vast tracks of time seem as featureless as the ocean after our ship has been and gone, its wake dispersed, water and sky as lonely as before, as empty. But the few steps to my grandmother's kitchen, to admire the Dutch tiles with the blue windmills and girls in clogs with starched caps on their heads, are bathed in light falling from the window on my left, and Minna stands with her back to the frosted glass, still with flour on her hands. She knows us all, Fräulein Minna, has been housekeeper since my mother was young, and so she is always pleased to see her or me.

Words too will suddenly melt into a white fog, just out of reach, an echo, a fading syllable drifting in mist, and it takes an effort of will, grasping and fumbling to retrieve it, the sound which goes with specific verbal intent, absolute meaning. And yet a childish song in an unused language will ring in the hollow of my skull for hours, flowers reassume the names by which I first knew them, and culinary flavours of my childhood refuse to translate.

The earth on which we move is circular, the horizon bends. Time, like memory, is a mystery, and in our beginning is our end. Holding my hand in hers, my child's child completes the cycle, leads me homeward. To where my grandfather sits in his armchair and takes his gold watch from his waistcoat pocket. Blow, he tells me, and it is my breath, I think, which flips open the lid. Although I cannot yet read its hands I listen to it ticking.

20

Adam and Eve were put into the world fully grown, so God the Father, like any caring parent, had to invent a childhood for them. It was called the Garden of Eden, and He must have known, as any father does, that they would eventually grow out of it, but He tried to make it last as long as possible, knowing that the real world, when they inevitably discovered it, was hopelessly defective, and that only death and disappointment lay in the future. He tried to keep them childish for as long as possible, and at first it was easy to dazzle them with colours seen for the first time, shapes and smells and tastes, the rising of the sun and the mystery of moon and stars. It was a world of plenitude, but full of hidden dangers for the newly born, and He kept a sharp eye on them, put down boundaries, and occasionally used his thunder to frighten them into submission, as fathers do. No doubt there is a trace of guilt in all this solicitude. Why did He create these creatures in his own image, conscious, endowed with powers of thought, knowing they were born to die, suffer and go back to dust?

What man or woman, thinking about parenthood, has not at some point asked the same question? Given the possibility of choice, is it right to bring a child into the world of suffering and death? Only those who still believe in the old religions are exempt from this dilemma. And yet instinct and biology still rule, despite qualms of conscience and the availability of birth control. We are being selfish, no doubt about it since, despite all the loving and giving we can offer, it cannot suffice. The happiest childhood must end.

Perhaps it is precisely for this reason that the craving for a child can be so strong. We find renewal in a newborn infant. Through it we re-enter the world afresh, as once we saw it, innocent, unadulterated by knowledge. For the joy of re-living, if only through another, the freshness of being, the glory of the world at sunrise, each shape and colour bright and beautiful. Where fun, amongst other things, is so easy to find, and laughter is innocent too.

And so we also tell them the stories in which we no longer believe, not only that Father Christmas flies across the sky and slips down the chimney, but that Jesus was born at Christmas and lay in the manger, whilst angels sang. As soon as they are old enough to sing a few ditties and lisp a sentence we dress them up as shepherds, Mary, the three wise men, and have them re-enact the story in which we are no longer able to believe, or do so only, for a moment, when seeing their angelic, innocent faces wreathed in tinsel and smiles. Adoring parents sit in the audience with tears streaming down their faces.

21

She wears her best dress, blue taffeta with lace trim on collar and cuffs. On her feet shiny patent leather shoes and immaculate white ankle socks. Her hair has been freshly washed and neatly pinned down. This is a special occasion. We step out of a taxi, mingle with the crowds milling about in the foyer, where I buy a big glossy programme from a smiling girl, and a box of chocolates from another attendant.

After a good deal of slow shuffling, our tickets are inspected by an usher and we are in the auditorium, a place of breathtaking splendour. Red plush seats, a high dome overhead, a myriad glowing lights reflecting gold paint. She puts her head back to stare at the wondrous dome, its far-off pattern, curious statuesque figures halfway between earth and heaven. How do they get up there? Nearby a girl takes her seat. She is wearing a dark red velvet dress, with a matching headband over a mass of black curls. My little blonde grandchild begins to scrutinize her intently, as though assessing the competition.

But the show is about to begin. The orchestra is tuning up in the pit, the house lights fade, the hubbub of conversation fades to a whisper. The orchestra strikes up officially, a rustic forest scene is revealed.

I can't see, she whispers urgently.

I lift her up on my lap.

A painted forest framed by the proscenium arch, two-dimensional flats, with no shadows. Lots of singing and dancing, and grown women trying to ape the gestures of children. Their songs evoke echoes of childhood, my father teaching me Gretel's songs. But there is more than a touch of religiosity in the lush orchestration. The forest of Parsifal rather than Grimm, cleansed of its ancient menace, barbarism. Instead sound and sight are imbued with a soft light of bogus sanctity.

In the auditorium row upon row of well-fed, neatly dressed children, their faces shining in the reflected glow from the stage, eyes sparkling. Small hands clapping, and a rush for the ice cream queue as the curtain falls.

When the performance is over the mood in the foyer is cheerful and matter-of-fact. High chattering voices, a fumbling with small sleeves and coat buttons, tying scarves and looking for the lost glove. Beyond the glass doors the street is dark, rain falling. I manage to get us both into a vacant cab. Fastening her seat belt, I heave a sigh of relief.

Soon be home, I tell her. What would you like for tea?

22

Only a story, we tell them. Riding home through rainy streets. Turning off the bedroom light, but leaving the door ajar.

Why do we keep such stories, of abandonment and child abuse, of cruelty and desperate hunger, even if prettified and set to music?

Why do we scare our children with witches, then tell them, when they wake screaming in the night, that they only belong in stories?

For there to be any sort of story, I tell her, in the cab going home, there has to be a bad bit in the middle, so that everything can come right in the end.

But this is also a fiction.

A few days after the opera matinee I read her the printed version, in that cosy hour of the afternoon when play has exhausted itself. I am using the original Brothers Grimm, but adding my own commentary as we go.

Gretel, I tell the child leaning warmly against me, was very lucky to have such a clever older brother. When the children, unable to sleep for hunger, overheard their parents plotting to take them to the darkest, thickest part of the forest and leave them to die for lack of food, or the hungry jaws of wild beasts, the little girl immediately gave up hope, crying bitterly. But Hänsel was a clever boy, and promised to find a way to save them both. Which he did, not once but several times, hoodwinking not only his parents but the wicked witch as well. Here, I think but do not say, was a boy with no illusions, a born survivor. As for Gretel, she was a fast learner and ended up as tough and ruthless as her brother.

I think, but do not say, that by the end of this horrifying story neither of them had anything left to learn. Is this a happy ending? The narrator, some ancient peasant woman, and wise in the ways of the world, clearly had her doubts. Custom requires closure, but the old woman could not disguise the irony in her version of events. So, with the stepmother conveniently dead, the children return to their monstrous father with enough jewels to keep them all living in perfect happiness. If you believe that you will believe anything, suggests the tough old granny who has seen plague, famine and civil war, as she concludes: 'My tale is done, there runs a mouse, whosoever catches it, may make himself a big fur cap out of it.'

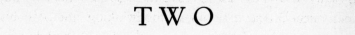

TWO

I

Once upon a time I was a child who lived happily from moment to moment, hour by hour. There was the routine of waking and sleeping, washing and dressing, going to the park and eating meals. My universe was made up of nursery and kitchen, living room and my father's office, outdoors and in. Summer meant carefree days at the weekend house, and sailing, winter involved frequent walks in the zoo. My world was peopled by a few permanent fixtures, parents, grandparents, the housemaid and the nursemaid, the fat washerwoman and the thin concierge. When my nursemaid was replaced it was a major event, which I did not like. I never forgave the newcomer for not being her predecessor, for being fair instead of dark, and quiet instead of jolly.

It did not occur to me that my life would ever change, or that it was restricted in any way. I moved in a world where shopkeepers smiled, and the policeman saw us safely across the road. I was curious about the peculiar building marooned in a sea of traffic at the end of our street. A church, my nursemaid said. I never went inside. Opposite it, on our side of the road, was a café with a terrace, tables and chairs. We did not go in there either, not ever. I had been in a hotel, but that was abroad, where we went for holidays. I had never been to a cinema, but my mother did magic lantern shows on the nursery wall on winter afternoons. If, when I started school, my mother took me to a gleaming white building in the suburbs, on a tree-lined avenue, it was obviously the best possible school. What other reason could there be? The occasion was duly celebrated, with a brand-new leather satchel and the traditional German *Schultüte*, a gold cardboard cone full of sweets and small toys. I was duly photographed holding it. According to custom and practice. Like every other child.

A child only knows what it already knows, especially when it has not yet learnt to read. Posters, signs, graffiti. It cannot feel excluded from the unknown.

2

Now, too, a sheen of normality over everything. I follow my routines of sleeping and waking, paying bills, answering letters. The earth continues to turn and there are signs of spring. Blossom scatters in the wind like confetti, drifts of snow on the pavement. A haze of palest green in the branches of empty trees. A promise unexpectedly kept. I rely on nothing, even though the trees keep burgeoning, buses still follow their accustomed routes, as do migrating birds, streaking across my skyline. I know that everything can be taken away within seconds, horror will catch out the unwary, but nameless anxiety is useless too. My radio speaks of global warming, extinction of species. My heart, on the other hand, craves rhythms. Fluctuations of light, wet pavements, night and day. The telephone ringing, and a child's voice speaking of birthday parties. Generations living out their lives in an orderly cycle, without fuss.

The children, I tell her, back from the forest, lived happily ever after.

Where is the forest? she asks.

3

The forest, I think but do not say, represents darkness, that which cannot be civilized, or brought under control. Cut down the trees, tame the landscape, but its shadow will always lurk on the edge of human consciousness. Without it, no history, myth loses its meaning. Magical presences, benign or sinister, waylay the solitary youth seeking his fortune. Human virtue is tested by old women, apparently destitute, in need of charity. Wild beasts prowl in its shadows, hungry for innocent flesh, particularly the sweet succulence of small children, lost and far from home. The forest is secretive, which is why so much is hearsay, strange stories passed down from father to son, repeated, with the odd fanciful exaggeration, by a woman warming old bones by the hearth, or scaring a wilful child into obedience, or simply whiling away the tedium of long winter nights. Someone remembers the blacksmith whose son set out on a journey and never returned, the miller's wife whose two small children vanished without trace on a bright summer's day, or the demented old crone who, years ago, gathered simples in the forest and would shout curses at anyone within earshot, and how several people, picking mushrooms or collecting firewood under the trees, had quickly died of a mysterious illness.

All this is ancient history. But the tradition continues, the heart of darkness still beats in its modern guise. Pistol shots ring out, echoing in the unseen spaces between rising tree trunks, lifting their canopies between earth and sky. Nobody sees, only the birds hear, as someone's child, father, daughter falls to the ground, never to be seen again. The earth covers them, falling leaves lie mouldering on the spot, signs of a massacre, deep in the forest, where leaves and children rot. Rumours abound, of course, in nearby villages, but it goes no further, not for the best part of half a century, whilst the peasants continue to go about their business, which is ploughing, animal husbandry, and so forth. Nothing to do with us, they mutter, not our business, not from hereabouts. Nobody's child, nobody's sister or brother, husband or son.

4

The afternoon sun slopes through my living room window, casting leaf patterns on the opposite wall. Pools of light gleam on the carpet, spill across her lap, catch tiny fronds of redgold hair. Everything seems solid, permanent. To her, certainly. She can think of it no other way except precisely so, the pictures on the opposite wall, the bracket clock on the old credenza where long-stemmed glasses look dusty and antique, the charms of the heavy grand piano, always tempting. I know that soon it will be dispersed, nothing is for keeps, but for her it will always stay like this, just as I see the potted palm by the window, my grandfather's bureau in the corner, the patterned tapestry draping the dining table.

She wants to look through my photograph albums. She wants to see what everything was like when I was a little girl, and the photographs will tell my story.

In every story there is a story which is not told. Nowhere more so than in the family photograph album. Every picture tells of a happy moment, or is made to appear so. Who knows whether the smile comes from within or is put on to order?

Who says the camera cannot lie? There they all are, the black and white snapshots, carefully mounted on dark pages, brightly caught images in a sea of forgetfulness, my father grinning at the tiller, my mother smiling coyly into the lens, but shielding her eyes against the sun, the extended family on a rare reunion relaxing on the terrace of a Swiss hotel in an aura of luxury and quiet leisure, apparently at ease, figures on skis and in bathing suits, posing cheerfully to hold the moment, hold it in perpetuity, as if conscious of the surrounding dark, the shadows inexorably closing in. Only the small children continue to occupy the moment, oblivious of the lens. My brother tries to fish a goldfish out of its bowl, I busily build in the sandpit, look for ladybirds in the flowerbed, nurse my doll in its cradle, assisted by the child who lives next door, eat ice cream with single-minded intensity, dig for worms with a stick.

For us, the children, the camera does not lie. Unaware of my father stalking us with his Leica, tiptoeing quietly, living totally in the moment which seemed to go on for ever, for me the pictures in the album concur with memory. As I talk, turning the pages, making sure her tiny fingers do not tear the interleaved pages of tissue, I can truthfully recreate happy moments, share remembered delights, small adventures, tell my story. This precious story of innocence caught in momentary snapshots, proof of a lost kingdom only I inhabited.

The story within the story. Or rather, my version of it. It is not often I can tell it to a listener young enough to get immersed in it too. She would like to join in my games, play with the toys visible in black and white.

I've got a sandpit, she says. And after a pause: It's nice. Will you take me there?

I can't, I tell her.

Suddenly I want to shut the album, suggest a game. The familiar ache has begun.

Why not?

I have already promised to take her to Venice and the Great Wall of China when she is old enough, so I realize that saying it is too far away would sound a lame excuse.

It's gone, I tell her.

What, the house?

I nod.

And the garden?

That too.

Even the cherry tree?

Yes.

She is silent for a moment.

We could go in a time machine, she says. And laughs.

5

The time machine waits in the dark. On some nights I have only to switch off my bedside light to be transported. It is not a journey undertaken voluntarily, for it brings no rest, murders sleep. But the cogs and wheels purr and turn, gather momentum, I hear my mother's footsteps echo down the corridor beyond the nursery door, kneel on the floor to watch how my grandmother uses a button hook to fasten the bar of her patent leather shoes, hear the sound of carpet-beating in the courtyard below. I cannot get back, trapped in a time warp, tossing and turning, counting the items in an inventory of loss, the streets, the mock gothic spires of the church marooned in a whirlpool of traffic, roses climbing up the nursery wall, the wooden boathouse by the jetty, riding the tram to school, everything. I am wandering in the dark, in the lost spaces of a world which belongs to the dark, ghost figures walk in its rooms, ride in the park, vanish into the church, ring the bell of the tram, stand behind the counter of a shop, sell fruit from a stall in the square, bring out winter coats for me to try on in an upstairs space which is carpeted and quiet, with sofas to sit on. I cannot stop, there seems no end to it, the doors which must be opened, lifts ascended, moments recalled, outings, presents given and long since lost, taken away, the washerwoman must be followed up the back stairs to the attic where trunks and suitcases wait to be packed for imminent departure.

6

Today I have chosen to read her the story of the wolf and the seven little kids. I feel it is relatively harmless, since only animals are involved, but remind myself that it is different for her, still in love with them, especially anything small and 'sweet'. I read out the warning the old goat gives her children concerning the wolf before she leaves them on their own. 'The wretch often disguises himself, but you will know him at once by his rough voice and his black feet.' She laughs when the wolf swallows a lump of chalk to soften his voice but gives himself away by showing his paws at the window.

Silly wolf! she exclaims. Then adds in a reproving tone: Their mother shouldn't go out and leave them all by themselves.

I explain that she had to go out and get food, and was too poor for a babysitter.

I get to the part where the wolf, to whiten his paws, first goes to the baker, who puts dough on his feet, and then asks a miller to powder them with flour. 'The miller thought to himself: The wolf wants to deceive someone, and refused. But the wolf said: If you will not do it, I will devour you. Then the miller was afraid, and made his paws white for him. Truly, this is the way of mankind.'

She pulls her thumb out of her mouth. What does that mean?

It means that people will often do bad things if they are scared.

So is the miller bad too?

Yes, I say. But not as bad as the wolf.

To get back to the text I repeat: Truly, this is the way of mankind.

And the further I read a story I only vaguely remember, the less it seems to concern the animal kingdom. Having begun, I have to continue, but I put my arm round her shoulder and stroke it as I read how the terrified little kids hid themselves, under the table, in the bed, another in the cupboard, but how the wolf found and devoured each and every one of them. All except the kid who hid himself in the clock-case, who survived to tell his mother when she came back to find the house in an awful mess, furniture toppled, bedding strewn on the floor, the wash bowl in pieces, and only a terrible silence when she called out the names of her little ones. Until she came to the youngest, and a voice answered from the clock-case. And you can imagine how she wept for her poor children.

Her thumb still in her mouth, cheeks flushed, she lets out a squeak of distress.

I tighten my grip on her for a moment and whisper: It's all right. You'll see.

I turn the page and there is a picture of the wolf, his stomach vastly distended, sleeping off his hefty dinner under a shady tree. And because this is a fairy tale she has an inkling. The little kids will jump out of the wolf's belly, unhurt, and they will fill his belly with heavy stones, stitch him up and watch him drown. On this occasion he tumbles into the well.

She extracts her wet thumb to grin up at me as I read out how the little kids and their mother danced delightedly round the well, crying: The wolf is dead!

The well, I think, but do not say, has been poisoned ever since. How will they live with it in future?

7

Where did she hide, all those years? In a cellar, an attic, or behind a door with a cupboard to conceal her space? I try to imagine it, the daily constriction of fear, I try to visualize her, my father's mother who had lived in widowed splendour for decades in an apartment too large for her, old furniture steeped in night, black dresses, a chauffeured limousine driving her from coffee morning to afternoon bridge, I try to see her, all of her children long since out of reach in foreign countries, most of her elderly cronies transported into the unknown, growing thin enough on meagre handouts of food to fit into a narrow space no larger than the clock-case which had stood for decades in one of the old-fashioned rooms laid out for a period in time which had gone for ever, though she failed to realize it, even as the wolf was baying at the door, smashing windows, burning, even as her children were fleeing the country, after her son had been swallowed up in the night and spewed out weeks later, a shadow of his former self, head shorn, emaciated and sick, bereft of laughter and curative sleep. I try to imagine it, the slow diminution, of things, pride, flesh itself, and then the last of her gold gladly handed over to die quietly in a foreign country where she knew nobody, humbly conscious of her lack of foresight, the futility of coffee mornings and afternoon bridge, her children and theirs a source of anxiety, unreachable. Lonely, sitting on a park bench in the summer of 1944, in an unknown city, watching Swedish children play. I look at them and think of you, she wrote, thinking of the six-year-old who was now twelve, translated to another country, speaking English. Worn out by the years in hiding, she died in her sleep a few weeks later.

8

A grey hamster who went by the name of Slipper was found dead in his cage this morning. He was her first pet, and at first she did not comprehend that the situation was irreversible. She poked his small corpse with a stick to make him stir, spoke coaxingly to him, offered him a chocolate drop. Her father came down and tried to explain. As he took the rigid body out of its cage she started to cry. To console her, he said that Slipper had gone to heaven. This at first did nothing to reassure or comfort her. Slipper was always very happy, she had looked after him properly, and could they take him to the doctor? She was not only upset but also angry: why should Slipper do this to her, with no warning? So her father explained that Slipper did not really want to go, but that God had decided that it was time for him to join his mummy and daddy in heaven, so they could all be happy together. He put the body in a cardboard box and suggested burial in the garden. A funeral.

This caused great excitement, an immediate change of mood. A patch of earth in a corner of the garden had to be chosen, soil dug up with a trowel. Afterwards the small mound was lovingly decorated with sea shells, glass beads, and a piece of slate on which his name was visibly scratched. In the afternoon I was told of the exciting event the moment I arrived, and she took my hand to show me the grave in all its splendour. Graves usually have flowers, I said, so we found a jam jar in the kitchen, filled it with water, and put in a few bluebells growing wild near the back fence.

9

There are no graves, no final resting places, so their ghosts continue to haunt the living. No stones, no actual date, no last rites to bring peace. Not so much as a piece of paper, an official death certificate. Ashes blown in the wind, fragments of bone, nameless, anonymous, in an unknown stretch of earth. And so the sense, always at the edge of consciousness, that those who have vanished are not dead, not really, but hover restlessly in a foggy limbo between earth and sky, waiting for those they love to find them and give them the gift of sleep. Oh to be able to lay my tribute of white flowers on a specific spot, mark it, and walk away. Let them lie, give rest to us all.

10

And so, a few days after the death of her first pet, I read her the story of the juniper tree. A tale of burial and resurrection. How a woman who longed for a child stood under the tree, paring an apple, when she cut her finger and blood fell on the snow. 'Ah,' she said, 'if only I had a child as red as blood and as white as snow.' How the snow melted and everything turned green, and then the flowers came out and trees in the wood grew thick, and the birds sang until the woods echoed and blossom fell from the trees, and the woman stood under the juniper tree and was very happy and ate the berries when they were ripe. But before the baby was born she wept and asked her husband to bury her under the juniper tree if she should die. The baby, a little boy, was born, as white as snow and as red as blood, and when she saw it she did die. Of joy, it was said. And so the husband buried her under the juniper tree, which was so near the house he could weep for her whenever he wanted, and talk to her too, and after a while he was more at ease and took a new wife.

I had chosen to read her 'The Juniper Tree' because, so far as I could remember, no one had ever read it to me as a child. The title attracted me, and a certain freshness, lyricism even, in the telling. And my own curiosity. A variation of Snow-White and Cinderella, I thought, and I could tell by her expression that she thought so too. She knew where the story was leading, and felt confident. Attentive, but pleasantly relaxed.

Stepmother time. We both knew what this meant too, or thought we did.

The second wife had a little girl, called Marlinchen, but although the two children loved each other very much Marlinchen's mother hated the little boy and was very nasty to him. One day when the boy came home from school she offered him an apple which was stored in a chest with a heavy lid, and whilst he was helping himself to the fruit she let the lid drop, and the boy's head was chopped off, and fell amongst the apples.

I am appalled by the words coming out of my mouth. Now I know why this story was never read to me as a child.

I think this is rather horrid. What about a different story?

Speechless, knees tight together, she nods. I fetch a jolly picture book and she sits quietly enough whilst I turn the pages, too quietly.

I shut the book with a cheerful, reassuring smile. Her face stays abstracted and solemn.

Can they put the boy's head back on again?

Do you want me to find out?

She nods.

Whilst I am finding the page I say: I'm sure it has a happy ending.

I am now wary of what lies ahead. I decide to skim over the bit where the boy's body is cooked into a black pudding which his father, unaware of what has happened in his absence, eats for supper. But now there is no head at all, only bones, which his sister puts under the juniper tree. Improvising, I tell her that the little boy's body was turned by magic into a wonderful singing bird, and the bird sang so beautifully that he was given presents, a gold chain for his father, a pair of shoes for his sister, and a millstone which he dropped on his evil stepmother, so it killed her stone dead. After which the bird was suddenly the boy once more and they all went into the house to eat their dinner.

You see, I told you. They all lived happily ever after. Where does it say that?

I I

Afterwards, when the child is no longer here, I marvel at so much horror transmuted into such beauty. The horror of the headless boy, the corpse propped up on a chair, his head kept in place with a handkerchief, the little girl deceived into thinking she has knocked it off, so easily duped into believing it was all her fault, a burden the young take on in all innocence when they love the victim, weeping salt tears as the boy is cooked and eaten. The deceived father, the distraught child, a woman conscious of an evil she is unable to control. And then light-heartedness, a drying of tears, the juniper tree beginning to stir itself, its leaves parting and coming together like a clapping of hands, and a mist rising from the midst of it, and the centre of the mist burned like fire, and the beautiful bird flew out of the fire, singing. Singing its song of horror, how his mother killed him, his father ate him, his sister wrapped his bones in silk and laid them under the juniper tree, but singing it with such beauty that all who heard felt light of heart, not grief.

The juniper was a healing tree. Seek its message, listen for its song.

12

She is an Easter child, born in spring, a symbol of resurrection. Her hair is pale as cool sunlight touching the bare earth and leafless trees, her eyes the colour of clearing sky reflected in a muddy puddle, indefinite, flecks of greenish brown, still translucent. We light candles for her birthday, one, two, three, and help her to blow them out. We cheer and sing, tell her to make a wish but keep it secret. Her wishes are guileless, granted easily, and as easily forgotten, and if not, the desires waiting for her are as multitudinous as stars in a deep night sky, although she does not yet know that a star is forever unreachable. A chocolate egg, a bauble, a magic wand. For the moment it is easy to make her happy. She is still too young to comprehend the cost of anything. A penny whistle is as good as a Stradivarius, better. Glass beads are precious, a paper crown will do.

In her we celebrate the rebirth of innocence. Green shoots bursting out of the bare earth. The return of light. Eggs gleam in bright foil hidden on ledges, in flower pots, beckon from a bookcase, a chocolate hare stands in for the pagan goddess who is hard at work in every park and garden, in every living creature.

We worship at the altar of her childish innocence,

bringing gifts. For the moment, we assume, it is easy to make her happy.

I wish I could fly, she says wistfully.

For weeks now, she has been saying: I wish I could fly.

13

The first Easter, and a different sort of resurrection. A cold spring morning, grey clouds scudding over rooftops and Hampstead Heath. Just off the boat, boarding in temporary rooms as gloomy as the March sky, my father, now too thin for his winter coat, his neck scrawny as a fledgling bird, has decided to hide our Easter eggs in the gorse hedges on the hilltop with the skyline of London visible far off, and scruffy heath falling away on either side of the horse pond with its dark grey water. It is too early and too wintry, and the spot is deserted. My father is being determinedly jolly, crying out each time I or my brother spot a chocolate egg rather obviously stuck in the prickly branches, but my heart is not in it, I am not enjoying this charade. I suddenly feel too old for this sort of thing. I do not know why I am in this cold, unfriendly country. I go through the motions of being a child, thinking: I wish I could fly back home. I am not yet seven years old. My father, too, is suddenly old, despite his play-acting, his cheerfulness. He wears his trilby hat to protect his head from the cold wind. It hides his shaved head: ever since he came back with his hair missing he has been much, much older.

14

Every loving parent tries to keep up the pretence of a perfect world for as long as possible. God put a high wall round the Garden of Eden in order to create the illusion of a safe playground for his children. Straight out of Dachau, my emaciated father hid chocolate eggs in alien bushes. But the dream was over, if he thought otherwise, he was kidding himself, nobody else. What Wordsworth called the light of common day had come with finality. A blanket of grey cloud covering this unknown city. Even in sunshine it was utterly different, not the light of innocence dancing on everything, in which I danced too.

How old is old enough for a child to know the world for what it is? In order to survive even the most mundane existence, by the standards of what we call the civilized world, a child must at some stage be taught not to touch dog shit, never to run into the road, not to go off with strangers. This last is particularly difficult to explain, since we do not want our offspring to think badly of the human race. In stories evil and wickedness is easily recognized, personified in a witch, a monster, someone with features of outstanding ugliness. What if you cannot tell? What if anybody could be bad, underneath? What if that nice man who looks like an uncle, who smiles and maybe even brings a sweet out of his pocket, is not what he seems? When and how do we explain, try to explain, about the existence of paedophiles, child killers, Dachau, men who wear brown shirts and armbands and high shiny boots, in short, everything that might or might not go on beyond the garden gate?

We think of this as a peculiarly modern dilemma. Not necessarily so, to judge from Little Red Riding Hood. She was not, after all, a town child, or a near-contemporary. A poor woodcutter's daughter, living at the edge of the forest when it was still wild, a natural phenomenon, untamed and dangerous. So was she more clued up than her twenty-first-century counterpart, did her mother warn her of the dangers lurking beyond the cottage door? Not a bit of it. We have her words just as they might have been spoken by a woman two hundred years ago.

'Here is a piece of cake and a bottle of wine; take them to your grandmother, she is ill and weak, and they will do her good. Set out before it gets hot, and when you are going, walk nicely and quietly and do not run off the path, or you may fall and break the bottle, and then your grandmother will get nothing; and when you go into her room, don't forget to say "Good morning", and don't peep into every corner before you do it.'

With or without her red velvet cap, a present from her granny, this is a little girl like any other, and her mother's voice is just as recognizable. Walk, don't run, mind your manners. Can I trust you to carry out this errand sensibly, like a good girl? Because little girls like to skip, jump, run ahead, pick wild flowers, and need to be reminded about being polite to grown-ups. So say good morning, and – interestingly – no prying in corners, implying an inborn curiosity. Not a word about the wolf prowling in the depths of the forest, whether on two legs or four.

So the question has to be asked: why not? The story-teller is clearly in love with her subject. 'Once upon a time,' she begins, 'there was a dear little girl who was loved by everyone who looked at her, but most of all by her grandmother, and there was nothing she would not have given to the child.' Hence the little red cap, which the child wore every day.

This is a story of childhood, of innocence and its fragility. Of the particular bond between the very old and the very young, living on the edge, sharing the moment. It is a special kind of love story. The wolf, anyhow, is always part of the plot.

15

Although the old woman came out of the belly of the wolf alive, she died shortly after her narrow escape. Unlike her granddaughter, she had been swallowed up some time ago when the little girl arrived, and the beast's digestive juices had already begun to eat into her ageing flesh. Her frail body seemed to collapse into itself, and the shock and terror of her experience caused her hands to tremble and her face to grow haggard, with dark staring eyes.

The little girl grieved for her, and continued to wear the little red cap long after it was really too babyish for a growing girl, and when it was far too small, instead of throwing it away, she put it in a drawer to remind her of her dead grandmother, and stroked the red velvet, and ran her finger over the neat little stitches which were so obviously a labour of love. If only, she thought, I had known of the wolf's wickedness, I would not have spoken to him as I did, but how was I to know, since nobody told me? And she would cry a little, and wipe her tears in the soft velvet, and whisper: I'm sorry, grandmother.

When she was old enough to ask questions, having reached the age of thirteen, she began – tentatively at first – to broach the subject, knowing how sensitive her mother was on this particular topic. She had, for instance, overheard bitter arguments between her parents in the days and weeks after her father had come to the rescue, saving both his mother and child in the nick of time. By now it was obvious to her that mistakes had been made, if only through lack of foresight. She did not wish to blame anyone for her childhood trauma, or even the loss of her beloved grandmother. She merely wanted to know why things had turned out as they did.

But when, finally, she thought she had found the right moment – she and her mother sitting quietly together in the sun, shelling peas – the girl was taken aback by the vehemence of her mother's response. In a bitter flow of words she began to speak of her mother-in-law in tones of unmistakable resentment. It was all her own fault, she said. For years I had been urging her to give up the cottage, come and live with us. But oh no, she was determined to stay put, hold on to her precious independence, as she called it, even though it was clearly not safe for her to live there on her own, and your father had to go out of his way to make sure she was all right, and chop wood for her, and all the rest of it. And once she got sick, what was I to do, with a newborn baby in the cradle, and a million and one things that needed seeing to, and hardly out of bed myself after a difficult birth?

I can imagine the scene between mother and daughter, even though it was so many years ago and was never recorded by the Brothers Grimm. I know how it would have gone all too well, because the little girl of my story, born into the twentieth century, heard her mother talk in much the same fashion in the years following the wolf's death. I know too that such conversations, involving, as they do, both recrimination and justification, a raking over the ashes, were painful for both mother and child. This girl who was a child no longer, unexpectedly caught up in the complexity of adult emotions: hidden rage, buried resentment, stifled guilt.

16

The fairy tale follows a definite pattern, rewards and punishment, escape from danger, and closure. That is its defining characteristic. The human psyche longs for it, which is why old women sitting by the hearth have been reciting such tales through the ages, whether dark or merely troubled. No play, whether comedy or tragedy, can end without it. We crave resolution, whether in marriage or funeral rites, and bring up our children to expect the same. Why else do we send them to sleep at bedtime with such stories, unless we think that closure will bring with it a peaceful night's sleep? The wolf is dead, hurrah. Now shut your eyes.

It is not so easy, even for children. Often they suffer from nightmares, with witches and wolves chasing them through the dark. Not every child can distinguish between dream and reality, or know when a story is merely a story. That, in itself, is difficult enough. But as day follows day, the life we have lived lengthens, and we begin to realize that there is no closure with nightfall, no end of the day with the closing of eyes and slumber, only the confusion of sleep and, with waking, sequels, consequences, a continuing of whatever has been, even if in a different form, as echo, reverberation, memory.

17

Every child has a history which stretches beyond itself, and she has already reached the point of knowing this. It happens so quickly. Every minute might be an eternity to her, but at the age of five she has understood that stasis is an illusion. However glorious the moment, a grain of sand, a leaf, the ladybird crawling on her finger, she knows it will pass, the insect will fly off, the leaf will fall from the tree when winter comes. From picture books and films she knows that once upon a time there were no motor cars, only carriages and horses, and women wore long dresses and curious hats. She knows that babies are born, coming out of their mother's stomach, somehow, and that old people die.

Since I qualify as old, this worries her. If I am unwell, it is necessary to reassure her. During a discussion on the possibility of my demise I point out that, whilst I may seem very ancient to her, I am in fact fairly youthful by modern standards. That if I live to the same age as my mother, she would be grown-up with children of her own by the time I died.

And your granny? she asks. How old was she?

I am speechless. This is the moment I have been dreading since she was born. Only it is not the moment. No, not yet.

Well, I say slowly, feeling my heart pounding as I search for words. That was different. It was during the war. They were killed. Both my granny and grandpa.

How?

The question comes quickly, too quickly. I am not ready for it.

I give the sort of answer my mother used to give, year in, year out.

I don't know.

18

It is not only children who need to be shielded from the truth. As I was growing up, long after I had grown up, my mother turned 'not knowing' into an art form. Even though, towards the end of the war, she had worked in a bureau dedicated to tracing the dead, the missing, the few survivors, she apparently achieved this self-deception. It continued for the remainder of her long life, almost fifty years.

But refusing to know is not an easy option. It gives the imagination too much scope, slithering helplessly from graphic horror to horror, documented by history, caught on film, visited in dreams. At one point, twenty years after the end of the war, when I had the temerity to ask, she told me that her father had been deported to Warsaw and met his death in an air raid. I knew this to be an impossibility, that no transports from Berlin had ever left for the Polish capital.

I do not know how long it took her to invent this fairy tale, or how long she was able to believe it.

I do know, however, that the fairy tale of the wicked stepmother took hold very soon and grew to monstrous proportions. Its roots dug deep, its branches overshadowed the past indelibly. So much so, my own sunlit memories of early childhood became an affront to her, could send her into a fury.

Often lonely during the war years, I liked to rummage through a box of loose photographs. It was a way of making contact with the past. Images of a lost world. My attention was drawn to a formal, full-length portrait of a woman in a long dress, style circa 1900, and I took it to my mother, to ask who she was. My real mother, she told me, who died when I was very young. I did not tell you earlier, since stepmothers in story books are always wicked, and I did not want you to love your grandmother any the less. To a child of ten, who now read fairy tales as a form of literature, I could see why she had acted as she did. As far as I was concerned, the woman I knew was my beloved grandmother, not this sepia stranger in a long dress, with her hair up. I put the unsmiling portrait back in the box with my other ancestors, their friends and relations. From time to time, shuffling through the snapshots, I might study her features, or ask: what was her name? Berta. Why did she die? In childbirth. Did the baby die too? Yes. How old were you? Three. My mother's childhood suddenly became romantic, like a story book. She had been sent away to relatives in the country, a place called Annaberg, where everyone was nice to her and she had a lovely time. I had read stories just like that, about orphans entering a new world.

But the child in my mother, the little girl lost, grew to hate her wicked stepmother. No magic could undo the harm, so in the end it was not a rifle shot, not poison gas or typhus which put an end to her father but she, the evil one, who refused to leave her home, put herself at the mercy of a stepdaughter who, perhaps, had always harboured an underlying resentment of the person who had taken her mother's place. How should I know? How could I know what went on when my mother was an adolescent, and later, except that it might have been no different from the difficulty between me and my own mother, which was hard enough, but without quite such harsh consequences, without anyone perhaps dying as a result.

In a world where cruelty has a human heart and jealousy a human face a wicked stepmother seems to be a human necessity. And once she is safely dead the teller of tales knows there will be no conflicting version of events. Humankind cannot bear too much reality, longs for simplicity and the comfort of closure.

19

I had tucked her into bed, read her the story of the musicians of Bremen, which is short and funny, and turned out the light. She has not yet outgrown her fear of the dark, so I left the landing light on and the door to her room ajar. I was about to go downstairs when she called me back.

Is there really a tooth fairy?

I know how it was in childhood, that sense of being surrounded by mysteries, fantasies, adults whose words were unreliable, so that the world of waking was very like the world of dreaming, a shifting of half-perceived visions, blurry outlines, cloudlike concepts hovering on the edge of everyday reality. She has begun to suspect that grown-ups do not always tell the truth, and that it is part of a game of which she does not know the rules.

I stand on the landing, hesitating, on the horns of a dilemma. I think it is wrong to lie to a child, but I am only human, enjoying the game which is her childhood. I think she is enjoying it too, and I suspect she would not thank me for telling the truth. It is only her intelligence which prompts the question.

Well, I say cautiously, as if treading on eggshells, if Father Christmas exists, why shouldn't the tooth fairy?

I put my head round the door of her little room as if ready to continue, if necessary. But she simply turns her head on the pillow and shuts her eyes, content to drift into sleep.

20

There is the lie direct and the lie indirect, used to shield children, and on occasion ourselves, from unpalatable truths. Faulty logic is a weapon in this armoury of deception and self-deception. The child wanted to go on believing in Father Christmas, to stifle doubt, just as human beings have for centuries used ludicrous syllogisms and all sorts of false premises to prove the continuing existence of God. A God moreover, who was good, even if this meant believing in Satan, and any number of specious explanations for earthquakes and other natural disasters.

The age of innocence goes with a belief in the benign nature of the world into which we have been born. I myself had early doubts of the existence of Father Christmas merely because I was told he carried a whip, not presents, for naughty children. How could a child who had known nothing but tender kindness believe in such a personage? I knew it to be just a ruse to make disobedient girls and boys behave themselves, and since nobody had ever laid a finger on me or my brother I guessed it was just an old-fashioned story.

I thought the rest of the world was also benign, but the moment came when the task of shielding me from the truth became well-nigh impossible.

*　　*　　*

Whilst I slept in my little white bed with roses climbing up the wall, the dark green blind drawn on the window overlooking only a quiet inner courtyard, buildings burned, every shop window in our street was smashed. By morning my father had vanished, apparently away on business, and my school had unexpectedly shut for a holiday, indefinitely.

It was odd, but not alarming. My mother was calm, and the nursemaid never had much to say anyhow. She was conscientious but boring. Her predecessor had been much more fun.

I forgot what happened when she took us out for our daily walk in the park, forgot it for years. Until, decades later, my mother told me of the lie indirect concocted for the occasion. On seeing the havoc in the street below, shopkeepers in long aprons sweeping up shards of glass, two children – aged four and six – were told: They are putting in new windows.

By the time we returned for lunch the street was tidier. Almost back to normal. Tidier, anyhow. The pavements, if anything, emptier than usual. A child's mind, just as tidy, undisturbed, a memory filed away for future use.

To lie forgotten until years later.

They are putting in new windows.

Everything is being made better. Now the street is tidy, empty of broken glass, nobody walks on the clean pavement, bright in pale winter sunlight. I remember my heightened curiosity as we turned the corner. What I saw was a return to normality. And now, lunch.

21

I'll huff and I'll puff and I'll blow your house down, threatened the wolf. It was a dark night, with the fogs of winter drawing in, and nobody now went into the forest to hear the birds or search for mushrooms, for the wolf had grown lean and dangerous and was no longer fearful of being seen in daylight, and it was known that he had developed a taste for human flesh. Men had left home to earn an honest crust for their family, never to be seen again. It had always been dangerous to go out of doors after nightfall in outlying parts of the city, with its unlit, lonely streets and patches of wasteland, but now even the most prosperous parts of the town, the boulevards, the residential streets of old houses with balconies and wrought iron gates, could no longer provide a safe haven for its rightful tenants. For the lone wolf was solitary no longer, but had learnt to hunt in a pack. In the dark each howl found an answering howl, and the bloodthirsty chorus could be heard from behind locked doors and shuttered windows, in attics and cellars. And frightened children were kept indoors, even during daylight, and told fairy stories with happy endings to calm their fears, but nothing could stop the terror if their house had been attacked, the windows smashed, the rooms ransacked, and daddy taken away after a beating. It was only the very young, the innocent, those fortunate enough to have seen and heard nothing, whose fathers had simply vanished, for the moment, though the moment would stretch into days and weeks, who could live out their brief childhood for a little longer, who could believe in the happy ending, that daddy would come safely home as usual, bringing each of them a present, as he always did. But as the days stretched into weeks, and nothing was as it had been, days growing darker, night longer, gloom spreading through every room, an eerie silence in what had been a happy home, a sense of absence, no visits, laughter, no school even, mother always out too, not in the mood for play, then these children too sensed, if only gradually, that life had changed for ever.

22

Her sense of stasis may have gone, but in its place she has a sense of order. What day is it? she asks. Or, what time? Her mother will pick her up at six o'clock. If it is Sunday it means school tomorrow. After fireworks and Hallowe'en everyone gets ready for Christmas, in the classroom and at home. Clocks, the big calendar on the kitchen wall, form a grid between her and chaos, the panic of not knowing what comes next.

We sing songs about the days of the week, read nursery rhymes about the changing seasons. January brings the snow. At Christmas time all Christians sing, to hear the news the angels bring. In April I open my bill.

I have a piano lesson on Saturday morning, and swimming in the afternoon. Shall I play you my new piece?

I open the lid of the piano, settle her on the stool, and wait. She makes several false starts, then manages to get through with only short hesitations.

Very good!

I am promptly given an encore. And a big grin. She slithers down from the stool.

What time is it?

Mummy is due in half an hour. Biscuits and a drink take care of the interim.

I remember how it was when all routine broke down. Dark November days with no school, just a sort of emptiness. The nursery full of books I could not read, nobody coming to play. Mother out since morning, father – where? Servants whispering behind closed doors, not doing their job of looking after me. Left to my own devices I tiptoed quietly through the unlit reception rooms, looking for clues. From the tall windows facing the street I saw life going on as if nothing had changed. Pedestrians hurrying through lamplight, black cars moving. The church at the end of the street had a Christmas tree, its coloured lights twinkling, above traffic level. I stared miserably at it. Christmas was happening without us. My mother, it seemed, was too busy with other things. Or had forgotten it. I felt forgotten too.

23

We've been to France, she says proudly. And I know some French.

Tell me.

We have been cutting out pieces of coloured paper, gluing them together. So far we have made a rocket and crown.

Bonjour, she utters emphatically, holding the blunt-ended scissors in mid-air.

It means hello, she adds, to enlighten me.

What about goodbye? I ask, shuffling the coloured papers. Can you remember?

She wrinkles her nose, looks up at the ceiling, lets out a heavy sigh.

Au revoir, I prompt.

I just forgot. But I knew it was O something. Can we make a butterfly?

Of course.

I begin to draw two large wings on pale blue paper.

How do you say goodbye in German?

Auf Wiedersehen.

She makes a stumbling attempt to mimic the words. A second attempt is nearer the mark.

The butterfly now has a fat body and two antennae.

Is that what you said to your granny when you came to England?

No. I do not remember saying anything. Only the empty apartment and my cry of childish anguish as the reality of departure struck home. Only the cortège of hired cars in the street, with my grandparents and an aunt in the rear and my father pushing me into the empty front car with its door already open, and the deathly silence as the vehicle pulled away from the only home I knew and the street I had always known and everything was receding with finality and my mother held her head in her hand and would not even look out of the window, and then, at the airport, no memory of words or touching or anything, just my grandfather peering through the window of the airport building trying, trying to see us, but failing, and my father with his mind set only on one thing: getting out.

I expect so. She gave me a brooch to remember her by.

But that was weeks earlier. When the reality had not yet struck my child's brain.

Can I see it?

Later.

Only my grandfather peering through the far side of the glass in his heavy winter coat of finest wool, hailstones starting to fall from the dark March sky on to his uncovered head, unable to see me inside the building, whilst his daughter and son-in-law had merged invisibly with the desperate crowd yelling at the officials behind the long desk. Set only on going, getting on to that plane waiting on the tarmac.

She has cut out the butterfly without mishap and is now waving it about in the air above her head. We decide to beautify it even further by sticking a silver star on each wing.

Schmetterling, I say.

I hang it in the window by a piece of cotton thread. We both clap our hands with delight. It looks pretty.

Schmetterling, I murmur.

24

Schmetterling, she says, apropos of nothing on her next visit. She is now learning to count: *Eins*, *zwei*, *drei*.

She wants me to teach her a nursery rhyme in German, and I put her on my lap for *Hoppa Hoppa Reiter*, though she is really too heavy to be bounced up and down on my knees.

Did you really not know any English when you came?

Not a word.

And then I remembered the unexpected lessons. How many were there – two? Three at the most? Time for a story.

Well, that's not quite true. One day our nursemaid brought us back from a shopping expedition, and as I was standing on the platform of the tram, waiting for it to stop, I saw our housemaid, Edith, standing in the street, waiting for us. She said we could not come in, but we had to go to my grandparents immediately. My daddy had come back, but he had something infectious, and was very sick. And whilst I was staying with my granny this lady would come to the apartment to give my brother and me English lessons.

What did you learn?

Not much. Napkin, she would say. Or table. Chair. And I had no idea what this was all about.

Didn't you know you were going to England?

No idea. And then one day it was time to go home, and when I got there all the furniture had disappeared, or most of it. And I was so astonished I hardly looked at my father, whom I hadn't seen for months, because the living room looked so funny with no carpets or chairs, and that's when he said, laughing and looking very pleased: We're going to England.

25

So many fairy tales involve a perilous journey from one land to another, where fortune waits. Luck and cunning are required, as wild animals acquire human form or, at least, the ability to speak, old crones repay a kindness, birds sing messages, and mundane objects have magical powers. Bribes are given and received, passwords spoken, transformations of identity are not unusual.

It was such a story. I never knew from one moment to the next what would happen. I was sleeping on my grandmother's sofa, then in a spare room of my other grandmother. Now my nursemaid was with us, but she had a terrible row with my grandmother. My mother appeared to settle the argument and vanished just as suddenly. I had never seen grown-ups yelling uncontrollably. I was intrigued.

I did not know from one moment to the next what would happen, but I trusted my parents absolutely. I had no idea why we were going to England. Perhaps it was an adventure, an exciting new start. Nevertheless I was puzzled. It seems we were going to a city which was foggy, where the houses were streaked black with soot. Why?

Wooden packing crates stood in the empty living room.

I had to choose which toys would go in. Bulky things had to be left behind. At night I thought of the weekend house, shuttered and deserted. My heart ached.

Mysterious rituals. Sitting in a cold grey corridor with loud male voices echoing from behind shut doors, waiting. To go into a room where a man in brown with an armband and boots sat on a podium with papers on his desk, looking down on us and asking questions. Then, on another day, sitting in a hallway with lots of other people, waiting to go into a room under the staircase where a man in a grey suit sat behind a desk and smiled at me.

Shopping for a new winter coat.

My mother took me into a sweet shop to spend my pocket money. I could not take the money with me. It was forbidden.

From now on we would be poor.

This was very odd.

I knew only stories where the protagonist went to another country to marry a princess and inherit a kingdom.

My mother was happy, my father was. I put my trust in them. They knew what they were doing.

Did you mind being poor?

She is counting toy money into a tin. We have been playing shops, and it is her turn to be the shopkeeper.

No, I laughed. As a matter of fact I rather liked it. It was like being on holiday. My mother looking after me, instead of servants.

Can I have some eggs?

I have already bought most of the shop contents.

All right, she says. That will be ten pounds.

When I protest she lets me have them for five pence, which is all I have left.

26

Normality is a delusion, the pattern of days and seasons. I learnt that at the age of six. Innocence will not survive such a violent uprooting. Childhood is a tender seedling, which needs nurturing. So, for over half a century now, I have been conscious of skating on thin ice. I have been lucky. Life's apparent normality is just a lull between storms.

So, another ordinary day. I wake up just after seven, draw back the curtains, regard the ever-changing English sky with suspicion. Sunshine at seven, rain by eleven. A patch of pale blue, but sullen grey clouds visible between the trees at the end of the garden. Could go either way.

I put the kettle on and think: Tuesday. No appointments today, just routine. I think about clothing. Will I be warm enough? Too warm? The news on the radio seems to be a continuation of yesterday's problems, so my mind wanders, picks up the bulletin in snatches, drifting off, drifting back. My body is uppermost in my mind on first getting up. Like an old car left in the garage overnight, it likes to show off its defects. Stiff joints could do with an oil can. If only.

I get on with things. Sufficient unto the day. Birth, death, hospital appointments. The expected and the unexpected, small triumphs and achievements, disappointment and failures, a bit of heartbreak, a bit of joy. Half a century of ordinary life, what is called normal, holidays and English weather, ever changing, ever the same, but nothing, nothing to cause a seismic shift, no earthquake, no abyss opening up at my feet.

I am conscious that nothing goes on for ever. Having had a sophisticated education, I am mindful of the Greek saying: call no man happy until he is dead. Not that I would call myself happy, but lucky, yes. I am doubtful about happiness, which I regard as a momentary by-product, like the rainbow, which comes and goes. But fortunate, yes, forever conscious of pitfalls, bolts from the blue, everything that can ruin a life from moment to moment. Or, as the poet says: teach us to expect the unexpected.

I was taught, very early.

Not in books. I could not read. Not in school. My first school had been shut down for ever.

27

She is curled up on the sofa, watching her favourite film, whilst I wash up the lunch dishes in the kitchen. Familiar songs are audible above the sound of running water. Oddly enough, although the film has been common currency, I have never actually seen it. Just the clip of Julie Andrews standing in a mountain meadow, singing, arms outstretched. I am not sure why I have never seen the film, since it is old enough to have coincided with my own children's childhood. Someone else must have taken them, and by now the film's immense popularity has made it something of a joke, so I have no curiosity about it. From the much-used soundtrack I imagine cowbells and edelweiss, blue gentian and the odd alpenhorn echoing between snowcapped peaks. The stuff of childhood holidays, in fact.

I pop my head round the door and she says: Come and watch it with me.

It is, I find, very important to her to have my company whilst a video is on. I do not know why, but she always asks.

I settle on the sofa, looking at the screen over the top of her blonde head, an arm round her. She pushes a raisin into my mouth, from the small box, the packaging as familiar as edelweiss.

I inhale the sweet odour of her body and see singing nuns, then a bevy of happy children in a lovely chateau by a shimmering lake, also a very handsome papa who has clearly taken a fancy to Julie Andrews, no longer wearing her habit but still looking a bit of a frump. She is only a governess, but she can sing, and all the children learn to sing too. I can see why my granddaughter is hooked on the film, since singing is her favourite thing, as natural to her as breathing. But now the Alpine idyll is threatened by the wicked stepmother, complete with designer wardrobe, lots of make-up and peroxided hair. Her smile is as artificial as the rest of her, but she is already planning to send all the children to boarding school as soon as papa has put the ring on her finger.

This is a true story, she informs me, stuffing another raisin into her mouth. Mummy told me.

Really?

It was news to me.

Potential stepmother sent packing, Maria is now marrying papa in a huge church, no, a cathedral. The other nuns, watching discreetly from behind wrought iron, look on with beaming smiles.

I expected the credits to start rolling, but no. Suddenly blood red flags with black swastikas on white spoil the cardboard scenery of picturesque streets, military vehicles roar over cobbles. The honeymoon is being spoiled by the Anschluss. Papa does not want to join the German navy, so they all run away over the mountains – after a last singsong in front of lots of people – and climb across the frontier, smiling happily under a blue and sunlit sky.

Was it like that when you ran away? she asks, turning her head to look up at me as the credits begin to roll.

Not really, I say. No.

28

No. Just a silent procession of black cars making its way to the airport, winding its way through busy morning traffic. Exit. Another exit. Just a grey cold morning, the northern light of a northern city, and a woman leaning forward, refusing to look out of the window as the familiar housefronts recede for the last time. Just an ordinary family of four struck dumb by this unceremonious expulsion from the city in which they were born and, at the airport, during the hubbub of passengers all trying to make their voices heard by the men behind the high counter handling exit papers, passports, valid tickets, the figure of my grandfather suddenly appearing on the far side of the plate glass running from floor to ceiling, trying – I could see vainly – to catch a last glimpse, but seeing, I think, only his own reflection, or at most a dark mass of people with their backs to him. All of them clamouring to get on the next plane, to get out of this city, to make their voices heard. I, only I, having nothing to do at this particular moment, stood staring out at the grey light and saw him, peering fruitlessly at a point above and beyond my head, and I tugged at my father's coat to tell him, but he just said curtly: Not now. I thought about banging on the window. When exactly? Then, or afterwards, when it was much too late? Time and memory are a plate glass window, no sound, no sight can go through in the other direction, however much I pound my childish fists on the frozen air and shout his name. Time and the moment have passed. It has begun to hail, the icy stones are falling on his bare head, on the shoulders of his overcoat. Hailstones bounce on the ground, fall out of the bleak March sky into the space between the window and the dark wooden wall two yards further, on to the blades of grass and asphalt between the base of the window and his feet, the no man's land where he has found this window, through which he cannot see us. I see him, for the last time. And then the space is empty.

29

So what was it like then, she persists, when you had to run away?

It is late afternoon. We are both tired, and I have run out of things to do, or the energy to do them. So, I think, has she. I glance at my watch, hoping desperately that her mother will arrive. Now. This minute.

Story? Something to eat?

She does not answer. I go to the window but there is no sign of the car.

Can I watch another film?

I explain that there is not enough time. Her mother should arrive at any moment.

Tell me about when you ran away.

I sit on the sofa and put her head in my lap. Her feet, in by now grubby white socks, stick up in the air on the arm of the sofa.

I try to turn it into a fairy story, spinning it out.

Well, I said, there weren't any mountains, so we couldn't climb them, could we?

She laughs.

And we didn't live by the seaside, so we couldn't go in a boat.

She shakes her head, looks up at my face.

I can see you upside down, she says.

I touch the tip of her nose with my index finger. How do I look?

Funny. I can see up your nose. Go on with the story.

So, if we didn't climb any mountains, and we didn't sail in a boat, what do you think we did?

She yawns loudly. To stave off the moment when she asks when her mother is coming, I put highlights into my voice.

We came in a *plane*.

Her eyebrows shoot up, her mouth opens.

Like when we go on holiday!

She muses, gazing dreamily out of the window. Her irises reflect sky, and cloud. The room is darkening. I ought to switch on the lamp, but postpone the moment. I do not want to disturb things.

Can I have a biscuit?

I hear the doorbell ring.

30

History has become myth, a fairy tale with a happy ending. I would like it to stay that way. Not yet, I think, not yet. Hold the moment, the precious moment of innocence. The world a glorious bubble shining in light, but about to burst. Hold it, hold it. God in his heaven and all right with the world. Just for a little longer, let her believe that mercy has a human heart, pity a human face.

I dread the moment of truth, of cruelty, terror. I want it postponed, held at bay indefinitely. Let her continue to believe in the fairy tale, the happy ending.

Schmetterling, she says on her next visit.

The paper butterfly is still dangling in my window.

Clever girl! I exclaim, unexpectedly moved.

Eins zwei drei, she adds.

A ladybird is crawling across the pane. I explain that they breed in my window frames.

Shall we let it out?

Eventually I get it on to her finger and it flies off.

She wants to know the German for ladybird. It is a bit of a mouthful, and she wrinkles her nose.

Can I draw one?

I fetch the box full of crayons and coloured paper,

spread everything on the kitchen table. I do the outline for her, and she starts doing black spots.

Your house is on fire, your children are gone, she recites, admiring her handiwork.

Mummy says, she remarks suddenly, crayon in mid-air, that you were very lucky to escape from Germany when you did. And we are very lucky too. Because if you hadn't she would never have been born, and then I wouldn't have been born either!

She beams at me, face alight.

I kiss her forehead.

THREE

I

The child sits on my knee with shining eyes. In them I see the world reflected, and it is dazzling. Through her eyes the world is bright at the edges, fresh every morning, cleansed in dew. She sees each thing in its particularity, as if for the first time. I know how it is, she reminds me. For now she embodies the world's delight. I watch with her as she looks with intensity at a dark beetle crawling up a blade of grass, counts off the petals of a daisy, sucks on a strawberry. She blows on a dandelion clock, or steps in a shallow puddle, and the moment is caught in an aura of absolute freshness, vivid, singular. Feathery down floats, water ripples and breaks, everything glows with colour, moving, stirring in the wind. Leaves whisper, grass sighs, a piece of paper floats right up to the blue sky where clouds float without making a sound, dry leaves scuttle into corners, noisily. The miraculous otherness of insects, ladybirds with hidden wings, busy ants, cunning spiders, the unexpected glory of a butterfly hovering in mid-air. The fast-beating heart of a small furry animal which can be held in the hand, stroked, invokes breathtaking solicitude.

I know how it is, having been what she is now. I know how precious it is, how brief the moment, which she finds endless.

The garden is full of sunlight, dappling in leafy splendour. I sit on the step with her and blow soap bubbles. Once or twice I manage to release a floating, iridescent sphere which gleams for a moment, before bursting into nothing. She only laughs, knowing there is plenty more liquid in the small container, enough breath left to recreate the moment, do it again, do better, let fly a shining cosmos and watch it go. I teach her not to blow too hard, show her how to flick the plastic ring so the bubble will float free, always a hit and miss affair. I enter into the spirit, vocalize surprise, triumph, passing disappointment, hope.

Through her I enter my lost world, forgetting how it burst. I see the world in a grain of sand, still a miniature gemstone, tell the ladybird on my finger to fly away home, her house is on fire, her children are gone. I teach her how to stamp on berries so they make a popping sound. Make her a daisy chain, discern a liking for butter by holding a buttercup under her soft chin. She picks up a feather, shows it to me, a husk, prickly on the outside, smooth within, an unripe berry, an empty snail's house.

Indoors we play with colours and shapes, simplifying the world. In my end is my beginning, and vice versa. She paints the sky blue, then sticks gold and silver stars on it. I fashion a cardboard crown for her to wear. The world grows smaller, and what is, is now. The moment is everything. The long journey behind me, I find myself back where I started, a homesick child. In the land with no future and no past, where the sun still glints through the tall trees at dawn, casting long shadows on the damp grass, as it did long ago. At long last, a traumatized child comes out to play, moving shapes and colours with ancient hands.

For a moment, with night coming on, I find the gift of timelessness.

2

But it has been hard going, getting to this point. Even now I am not sure I am out of the wood, with its lurking terrors, wild beasts howling in the night. I sit in the Odeon and watch the horror unfolding. I sit in the dark – was it yesterday? – and watch the living dead, the tottering skeletons, the heaps of unburied dead. I sit by myself with the black and white images flickering on the huge screen and realize that everything has changed for ever, that the world I am about to enter is not as I thought it would be. I sit by myself, watching the mute eyes from hell staring back at me from the hollow sockets of shaved skulls, far too heavy to bear, the heavy skulls, for fleshless necks and bone-thin shoulders, far too heavy to bear, the knowledge in those dying skulls, and know that now, on the brink of victory, on the verge of adolescence, the difficult years of childhood and wartime coming to an end, the world I was about to enter, re-enter, with April sunlight on suburban streets, was changed for all eternity. I came down the steps of the Odeon, blinking in the too-bright light of a Saturday afternoon, and everything was suddenly distant, alien, the quiet English streets, everything uneventful under an empty sky.

I had lost my tongue. I could not speak a word of the

language I had learnt so assiduously. I felt it was all a lie, the bank on the corner, the municipal flowerbed, the bus stop opposite the haberdasher. What had I to do with this pretence of normality?

3

Something opens, something shuts. Remember, this is not yet history: this is now. This is not war as I have understood it, living with it for six years, air raids, news bulletins of soldiers wading ashore, tanks rolling, happy women waving, throwing flowers. This is a secret at the heart of darkness opening up, a yawning stinking pit. This is Hell, no longer mentioned in religious instruction, whether at school or in the Girl Guides: no need to frighten the children with medieval notions regarded as ludicrous since the Enlightenment. Nor is this a grotesque political cartoon, to remind us what we have been fighting for, or against, for so long. No, nobody was fighting to stop them dying so unspeakably, for nothing. What had this to do with rockets, tanks, North Africa or Monte Cassino? There will be no victory celebrations, not now.

Something opens, something shuts. A hidden wound opens, a dark pit, deeper than any bomb crater I have peered into up till now. But human lips shut. That which cannot be spoken must be left unspoken. I rode home on the red double-decker which duly stopped opposite the haberdasher and, following its usual route, let me alight at the top of our street, I turned the key in the lock, entered, but did not speak. My mother did not speak either. The silence went on and on. We circled round each other, doing what ordinary people do on a Saturday afternoon, just for something to do, to avoid speech. Both of us avoided looking at each other. The silence grew deeper and more terrible.

4

Afterwards, many years later, this story shocked those who heard it. I had been sent, as a child, just thirteen years of age, to view the horror. Was I still a child? I do not know. In any case, I was unaccompanied by an adult. No doubt my mother had seen the appalling newsreel earlier in the week. Struck dumb, I never asked, she never said. Would it have changed anything if she had sat beside me, a loving parent, and held my hand in the dark? I might not have felt, as I did, that I was being punished, not for any particular misdemeanour, but simply for being myself, young, ignorant, self-determined. I doubt whether I would have felt less guilty. I also question whether my mother had the strength to put herself through it a second time. She knew, as I knew, that her father and stepmother were dead, together with uncounted others, cousins, aunts. This, this was our story. Now you know.

How do you confront a child, if child it is, with what is not history, but of the moment? Today I might have been refused admittance by the cashier or an usher, but this was a newsreel, even if nothing else was showing. Unlike previous newsreels, the keep-your-spirits-up tone was missing, no cocksure commentary, no hint of triumphalism. Nobody, not the most hardened soldier or commentator had expected to confront anything like this.

How old is old enough? Today's children are not admitted to the Holocaust exhibition at the Imperial War Museum if they are under the age of fourteen. In the spring of 1945 I was sent, by myself, to see the newsreel of 'liberated' Belsen. Was there any way of softening the blow? Should any attempt have been made to do so? I have since heard that in some schools entire classes were marched to the local cinema to witness the hidden crimes of the enemy. Nothing to do with propaganda, since the war was finally won. It was a lesson, but not part of the timetable: a lesson in something new. Just as Hiroshima, a few months later, would break every concept of what was, and was not, possible.

It would have been different for those other schoolchildren. It was not their story. It was the missing part of mine.

5

In my school, nobody spoke of it. In history, I did the three-field system and Magna Carta. Later on I did political history, which ended with the Treaty of Versailles, with no mention of its consequences. During a geography class the girl sitting beside me said Germany had done a good thing in getting rid of the Jews. I told her to sit elsewhere in future. In science lessons we continued to be told that atoms were indivisible, though the teacher laughed with embarrassment. Everyone knew our textbooks were out of date. Our headmaster taught ethics to the sixth form, using only Socratic dialogue.

As for the silence, nobody broke it.

Jewish refugees, so lately enemy aliens, applied for British citizenship and were naturalized. Naturalization was the word for it. My first passport, issued in 1946, states: British subject by naturalization Imperial Certificate No BZ1529 dated London 7 June 1946. In the photograph I resemble Anne Frank, except that I am wearing my British school uniform. And I am solemn, not smiling.

Girls of fourteen often study themselves in the mirror, and this is the expression I recollect. Unsmiling dark eyes. In class, I would fix my gaze on a teacher and see them avert their eyes, as if in discomfort. In the mirror, I felt I was staring into a dark pit. I thought others saw it too.

In fact, my camouflage was convincing. I had adapted well to my new habitat. I was consistently top of the English class, could please the teacher by writing essays in any required style. My accusing eyes were mere self-image: old school reports speak of a girl who is obviously clever but inclined to take things rather too easy, having proved to herself and everyone else how easily she could do whatever was required, listen with half an ear whilst reading a library book under the desk, staring out of the window, entertaining her friends by reading out an unbelievably soppy essay which she knew, rightly, would get her a top mark from a gullible teacher with no feeling for the hard edge of truth. Knowing she could and would always catch up, if and when she wanted to, and leave school with the necessary bits of paper.

Nobody saw into the dark pit or, if they did, chose to ignore it.

6

But then the dreams began. Recurring. Always the same dream. Back at the airport, waiting for take-off. Through the window, as if through the wrong end of a telescope, a tiny group of figures, at the edge of the field. Waving. The point of departure.

Day and night. The conscious mind and the unconscious. I read Freud and Jung, analyzed symbols, applied critical theory to poetry, pondered the validity of the objective correlative. I wrote on the collective unconscious in relation to Beowulf, immersed myself in the sea imagery of Shakespeare. I wrote poetry which had nothing to do with me, everything to do with my reading. I put my hair up, bought a long cigarette holder, aspired, on my student grant, to dress like a Left Bank existentialist.

At night I slept soundly, except that the dream would recur, a familiar loop of film. Airport, tiny group of figures, waving. I looking through the window, the immense empty field, only those figures at the far end.

Got up in the morning, did not think about it. Thought about a poem I was trying to write, using the image of red and black poppies, petals dropping in a field of corn, a conceit linked to Ceres and Persephone.

I put on a new lipstick, rehearsed a winning smile in the

mirror, which did not reach my eyes. I thought about existential angst, my new earrings, sexual allure and how to use it, and the question of modernism in relation to poetic language. I was inclined to dismiss the Freudian interpretation of dreams as ludicrously phallic. I believed in exercising the critical faculty: I thought I was being taught how to.

At night I slept soundly, through the dream, about which I spoke to nobody. I did not write a poem about it. I had shut it off, behind a wall of speechlessness. Hidden in the dark irrationality of night. It had nothing to do with the English literary tradition. I was a parrot, clever, but a parrot. Mouthing my English phrases.

It was only later, having graduated, that I began to read further afield. Kafka blew everything apart. What had rationality to do with anything? Studying his photograph, I saw my own eyes staring back at me.

I attempted to understand the incomprehensible, buying a copy of Raul Hilberg's *The Destruction of the European Jews* as soon as it was published. It was 1961, the dream had reached daylight, I wrote, when I wrote, of nothing else. I had turned round the telescope, now those tiny waving figures had grown, perhaps out of all proportion, blocking out the horizon, not waving now, no. They never left me.

I read, when I read, every last footnote. Figures, the bureaucratic machinery of death. Logistics of killing, organizational structures, industrial complicity, officialese, documents, everything. Cold, matter of fact, relentless methodology. History, and a historian, ruthlessly in control.

To know, but not to know. Separating the private from the public knowledge, that was something else. The mind is very clever about knowing everything, and knowing nothing, both at the same time. It has taken me a lifetime to acknowledge it, try to close the gap, look up records, put names and familiar faces on to a specific railway wagon on a particular day in the spring of 1942, attempting to follow those beloved faces on the last stages of their journey, broken at Trawniki, a little known transit camp, until first one, and then the other, set off for the final stage to death and dissolution, the ultimate barbarism.

The unimaginable is a fearsome thing. It spawns a Hydra-headed monster which cannot be laid to rest. The images keep coming, no sooner has one been dealt with than another possibility takes its place, worse than the first. And so the human mind splits itself in two, the intellect becomes adept at keeping wild imaginings in check. It reads textbooks, studies the data, the industrial processes of genocide, the recycling of gold and clothing, human hair and dental work. The rational self seeks to understand, almost as a necessary duty, how human beings apparently like ourselves could sink to such depths, how an entire society could condone, at least become complicit in the cold-hearted murder of the old couple next door, or the children who used to play in the courtyard below, their innocent voices echoing between the walls and rising rows of windows. The rational mind seeks to measure degrees of complicity, from sadism to cowardice, from unbridled greed to opportunity, furniture bought on the cheap, a flat unexpectedly empty, a gold ring set with diamonds for a favour which cost nothing, to self-delusion in its multitude of forms, prolific too. Knowing nothing. Euphemisms about resettlement, work camps. What could I do?

The rational self seeks to comprehend the incomprehensible. In order not to demonize evil. But reason loses its grip in sleep, and history repeats itself, helplessly. The dead are waving goodbye but will not let go.

7

Not to demonize evil. Not to fall into the same trap, racist, unthinking. I am a civilized human being, and conduct myself with civility. I go out of my way to be polite to a German visitor, conscious that she is conscious that I am being magnanimous. When a third party reports back to me that the visitor had been deeply impressed by my behaviour I affect surprise. Why? I ask with mock innocence. You know why, she says, and of course I do. I have been play-acting, up to the hilt. She seems a pleasant woman, my mother's age, and we are staying in agreeable English surroundings, immersed in the study of Shakespeare and his age.

It would continue, this delicate balancing act, walking the streets of my childhood, uttering my mother tongue, each step fraught with difficulty, treading on eggshells, overstepping sharpened swords. Not everyone was as circumspect, as grateful as the nice German woman. If they saw the shadow, if they guessed, they chose to ignore it, apparently as detached, as indifferent as they had been whilst the most heinous crime in history was being perpetrated under their noses, by their kith and kin, in their name. Possibly with their approval?

I do not ask. I keep up the pretence of civility, of

being merely a tourist. I feel they are only too happy to collude with the play-acting, avoid the awkward question, the whiff of sulphur and brimstone lurking under our feet.

8

I think I know only too well what it is I cannot bear to tell the child who sits on the edge of the world with fresh, shining eyes, golden hair gleaming.

But perhaps it is my problem, not hers. Perhaps she will take it all in her stride, absorbing what is the history of the world, receding into the past, along with the Black Death and the feudal system. Insofar as my story is also hers, she will still see it as, personally, one with a happy ending. One which enabled her to be born.

Can one separate light from dark, night from day, fear and joy? She sits on my knee and I tell her fairy tales, grim but redemptive. I am the voice of an old woman, echoing down the ages, keeping fearsome shadows at bay. The voice tells story after story, theme with variations, as night closes in on the loneliness, as the wolf howls in the secret heart of the forest, and the child whimpers for fear of the rising wind, imagining terror in the dark beyond the door. It is not only the wakeful child who needs the right sort of story before falling into the shadowy chaos of fitful dreams, but the child in all of us who longs to hear, once more, how the hungry cruel wolf is outwitted, once more, how his victims jump out of his belly, yet again, without a scratch. How bones long since buried sing their song until the spirit rises up in the form of a bird and the murdered boy reassumes living flesh. In despite of wickedness, of malice, innocence and goodness will survive. Stepmothers die horribly, the wolf drowns with his belly full of stones, witches burn to death in their own ovens. Cruel sisters end up crippled, humiliated, their eyes pecked out. The soul is a bird, a free spirit, it flies from the tree under which the murdered boy's bones lie buried, singing his story, finding revenge and resurrection. When their father rode to the fair Cinderella chose, not clothes and jewels, but the branch of a tree to plant on her dead mother's grave. And the soul of her mother flew from the hazel tree, which took root, in the shape of two white pigeons and a couple of turtle doves to help the unloved girl to achieve happiness, to bring down all the birds from the sky to help her fulfil the task of picking lentils out of the ashes, to clothe her in a dress of silver and gold, and, on the very threshold of the church door, to peck out the eyes of her false sisters on the wedding day.

It is as old as history, this myth. It needs no teachers, ignores religion, is deaf to dogma. Its story is told on the wind, whispered in the branches of trees, etched in the night sky. We are ashes, we are dust, but so is the bird which flies skyward, singing, singing. It is part of us, this cycle, resurrection, metamorphosis, a skeleton bursting into leaf, green as mystery, silence turning to song as a dead bird soars to a blue heaven. Scatter our ashes to the wind. If we are part of this cycle, let us fly.

The Holy Ghost is depicted as a bird.

I sing, silently, and with an aching heart, a nursery rhyme of a bird carrying a message from a far-off mother, to whom only the bird can return.

9

Running too excitedly from room to room, she has collided with the furniture and banged her head. The tears flow, the howling starts, suddenly, with a promptness which should not, but does surprise me.

I sit her down on my knee and propose to exert my 'granny magic'. She quietens down immediately, knowing its efficacy from long experience. It involves a rhyming chant, ordering the pain to go away, accompanied by a slow, very slowly circulating finger round the spot where it hurts, finishing off with a puff of breath, repeated thrice, to blow off the dwindling ache.

Better?

She nods solemnly.

Fully recovered, she declares that I actually do look like a witch. I look fierce, wave my arms about, and pretend to chase her round the room. Screeching with pleasurable fear, she takes refuge under the piano. I give up, partly because I am too old to crawl with ease, but also because I sense that, cornered, the pleasure will give way to high-pitched panic.

Fright is fun, but only up to a point.

Where the point is: that is the mystery.

When there is no escape route, nowhere to run? In the

shifting reality of her world, I might change shape, just like a Disney cartoon, or an old crone in a story. I might really gobble her up. You never quite knew where you were with grown-ups, when the pretending might stop, turn into something else.

10

The child is both my redemption and a source of anguish. Her existence, or rather, my relationship with her, stirs too many memories. I did not have a grandmother for long and now, adopting this role in my turn, I am forever conscious of her ghost. I play my role in her young life, my last, but the scene is full of shadows, disturbing echoes. I am not only myself, grown old in turn, we move in harmony, her movement is my movement, my heartbeat hers, reverberating down a dark tunnel of years, awareness of her loss informs my gestures, the part I am now assigned to play in this child's life, but with no martyrdom. She is both my sunshine and its shadow, and I am also conscious that I will be taken from her, though not, thankfully, in such traumatic circumstances. Let her grow up, able to regard my going as simply nature's cycle.

Give her a calm temperament, and an absence of history.

I give her a gold necklace with a jewelled pendant. Wear it on your wedding day, I say. She runs to a mirror to admire herself. Smiling happily, turning her head to varying angles.

I give the present lightly, without solemnity. But I am thinking of another gift, my grandmother coming through the folding doors between dining and living room, holding a brooch in her hand. A garnet rose, dark red, which I took without thinking, childishly pleased with the pretty thing. Proudly showing it to my mother when she came to pick me up. Oh, she said admiringly, as grown-ups do, kneeling to button my coat. Was that the very last time she came to fetch me from the familiar apartment, home from home for as long as I could remember? I knew and did not know. I knew, dimly, that this was a farewell gift, but had no inkling as yet of its finality. For the moment I was just proud of the unexpected present.

I I

The young regard life as an outward journey, losing the past. They fix their eyes on the far horizon, the hazy shimmering point where sky and ocean meet in the morning sun. They leave behind, they think, the ruination of their ancestors' lives, the bombed-out cities, shabby marriages, the endless make do and mend, the hopeless lack of aspiration.

Looking out to sea, the future is an ocean without a mark, reflecting an endless sky. Nothing is sure, definite, only that the point of departure will recede, drop out of sight behind us, dwindle to nothing.

The emptiness is freedom, possibility.

Self-invention. No history.

What is lineage? The wake left by the travelling ship, fading to nothing.

Look ahead, to the future. The horizon is clear, now misty, but forever empty, waiting.

Bit by bit I will fill in the emptiness, select, reject, pursue, say yes or no, find that which I am looking for, or keep on trying.

I am an existentialist, a child of war. I wear black, but not in mourning.

My eyes are fixed on the future. I will carve my life out

of the empty air. Create beauty, seek the moment of rapture.

But the earth is a sphere, and a voyage must end where it began.

The ship kept moving forward, and the journey was, on the whole, satisfactory. Interesting ports of call, minor squalls, but enough landmarks, sufficient highlights to sustain a sense of meaningful progress. By and large I felt I was going where I wanted to go, that I had also been lucky.

And then, suddenly, I was back where I started. Appalled, distraught. A child living the horror. But a child who knew, bereft of innocence, carrying the weight of a lifetime's knowledge.

12

I can't wait to be eighteen, she declares fervently.

Soon enough, I say. Don't be in such a hurry.

But I remember the intolerable slowness of hours, day following day.

She is playing at dressing up, teetering about in my shoes, which her small feet only half fill. A sliding motion, so the shoes will not fall off. A brightly coloured scarf draped round her neck trails the floor. I have a box full of outdated trinkets and she puts on a pair of clip earrings, but soon takes them off because the clips pinch her lobes.

Can I keep the beads?

Yes, I tell her.

I'll do whatever I want. It's the law − when you're eighteen.

She prances about the room. One shoe drops off, and she steps on the end of the scarf whilst trying to retrieve it.

Oof! she laughs.

So what will you do?

She stands still, head to one side, considering.

I'll go to bed whenever I want, even if it's the middle of the night.

13

A sense of growing unease, that is how it began. The voyage – continuing the metaphor – was not going as expected. I had been looking forward to fresh landscapes, unexplored coastlines. Into the sunset, glowing in the west, a dying ember, but also a new experience.

Instead I began to recognize familiar outlines looming closer, ever closer, throwing long shadows. As for the horizon, it was utterly obscured. The prow was no longer headed outward, cut off from the land, but hemmed in by an ever narrowing harbour. To say that I was upset is an understatement. I had not come all this way, using so much initiative, simply to find myself back where I started, under cold northern skies, indefinitely stuck in a cul-de-sac. I felt like a traveller who had inadvertently bought the wrong ticket, made a foolish error. I had doubts about my own sanity, but could find no way out, no escape, re-routing. I was trapped in my own skull, spherical as the globe, with nowhere left to go.

Half-demented, I wept with a ferocity totally alien to me.

How could I be so stupid, so deluded? I might have

been a flat-earther, unexpectedly back in his home port with nothing to show for it.

The future runs out, the clock runs backward, taking us back to the starting point.

14

Snow-White, a stout dowager queen in her regal apart-ments, lies sleepless in her four-poster, whilst the lady of the bedchamber rests across the threshold, snoring lightly. The old Queen tosses and turns, rumpling the silken sheets, hearing the owl hoot in the royal hunting grounds, which stretch mysteriously into the night. The casement is firmly shut, but night after night she hears it and, whether sleeping or wide awake, she runs in terror through the dark forest, stumbling over tree roots, catching her gown in thorns and branches, skin torn, fingers scratched and bleeding, but conscious only of her own heartbeat, the uneven sound of her own breath going in and out, seeing only the huntsman draw his knife. Draw his knife. Lifting his arm, then telling her to run for it. And herself running through the dark wood, full of predatory beasts lurking, invisible mouths ready to devour her.

Where are they now, the years of wine and roses? It is as though the good years had never been, the prince on his white charger, first love, regal splendour and happy domesticity, the first child long since grown to manhood, his father laid to rest in the family crypt, alongside his ancestors. The glass coffin is down there too, a memento to her beauty, but she has left instructions for it to be shattered on her death, the shards buried in the forest. The child in her, the young girl of such beauty, is out there already, terrified, running for her life, every other memory dim now, deprived of meaning, lost in the loop of time. But the forest is changeless, looms large in her loneliness, whispering her story night after night. The hollow cry of the owl mocks illusory happiness. Far off in the depths of the forest a wolf howls to the furthest star, hungry for blood.

15

She is not little now, and it is many years since she wore the red velvet cap her grandmother made her. The nickname she bore as a child is only a part of her personal mythology. Needless to say, it does not appear on her passport. The fact that she has a passport is an important part of her story.

She is a grown woman, with children of her own. With them she speaks a different language.

She has brought them on a visit, to see where she was born. With them she speaks a different language, but memory uses another vocabulary. She tries to keep her tone light, evoke carefree fun.

They do not see what she sees, since the place has changed out of all recognition.

The forest is now a park, with clearly marked footpaths, litter bins, and a picnic area.

No wolves, needless to say, only birds and squirrels. The children sit on a bench and swing their legs. We used to pick mushrooms, she says.

A man walks by, with a large dog. The children draw back, but his owner pulls him in by the leash. A notice-board by the entrance had warned about keeping dogs under control.

The children play hide-and-seek, but do not stray far. Also under instruction.

After a while she takes the children, one by each hand, along a narrow path overshadowed by bushes. She has to bend so as not to snag her hair in branches. It leads to a derelict cottage, roof partly open to the sky, a splintered door lying half buried in nettles, no windows, signs of burning in the ruins. The old hearth and chimney breast are still recognizable, the narrow stack pointing to a patch of sky.

She is suddenly silent, very still.

The children look up, slightly puzzled. Something about her expression makes them speechless.

She picks a few wild flowers growing in the ruin and puts them in the blackened hearth.

After a few moments she says: time to go.

Gripping each child so tightly that their fingers hurt.

16

Sometimes it is better to be an orphan. The fortuitous death of the stepmother during Hänsel and Gretel's absence only made things worse. It meant that there was no convenient scapegoat to blame for their terrible ordeal, and the father stood exposed for what he was, a weak, contemptible and cowardly man.

Hänsel, always resourceful, a born survivor in a wicked world, no longer had either respect or affection for his father, who soon gave up any attempt at parental authority. Little Gretel looked to her brother for guidance, as she had done during their terrible ordeal in the forest. It was the boy who kept control of the jewels they had brought back, disposed of them from time to time, and decided how the proceeds were to be spent. He instructed his sister to keep their father adequately fed whilst he himself was out of the house, and once a year he would buy him a new suit of clothes at the country fair.

Conscious that he had forfeited any right to respect, the father took to drink, which would make him maudlin with self-pity. Hänsel was content to let him destroy himself, and he was often a sorry sight. In the boy's absence the father tried to wheedle favours out of his daughter, and made clumsy attempts to win back her affection. His attempts came to a climax one Christmas, when he cut down a fir tree in the forest, set it up in the house, and decorated it with gingerbread figures given by a neighbour who was inclined to feel sorry for him. The girl became hysterical, and shut herself in her room for several days, refusing all food. When Hänsel came back and saw what had happened he took a cudgel to his father, beat him black and blue, kicked him out of doors and left him in the snow overnight. He died of cold.

Gretel never married, but kept house for her brother, who became wealthy, slowly and surely, trading on people's desires. They kept themselves to themselves, which led to a certain amount of gossip. But no child was ever turned away from their door. The hungry were fed and the homeless were given shelter, whilst the unloved found unexpected kindness.

17

What happens to a girl who, on the brink of puberty, sleeps for a hundred years? She is not immune to dreams, and dreams measure the passing of time in their own way, which is both more truthful and more surreal than waking time, the counting of clocks and the cycle of seasons. For a hundred years she has been tossing and turning, falling into dark cavernous spaces which bend and stretch, change shape and suddenly collapse, running from the fearful fantasies of childhood, picking flowers which fall to bits between her fingers. And every now and then she hears it, the turn of the spinning wheel, the hedge growing ever higher, the walls of the old castle creak as thorny briars take hold, clutching ever tighter, strangling daylight and undermining the strong foundation. She knows, through her sleep, that her finger still hurts, will go on bleeding, will never heal, however smooth the skin. And, as she tosses and turns, going on multiple journeys which are always part of the same journey, she hears the old woman's wheel turning and knows that the thread she spins and the thorny shoots of the hedge holding her and the world into which she was born imprisoned are one and the same. Now and then a glimpse of daylight. Briefly she sees a golden ball glittering in morning sunlight against a clear blue sky, but when she tries to catch it her arms are heavy as lead, will not lift, her longing is strong but the pull of the earth holds her down, relentless. And so she dreams, visions of glory, visions of hell, gradually recognizing even as she sleeps, that every glimpse of release is only an illusion, and that the submerged world through which she travels has neither logic nor progression.

The hedge might part of its own accord, the kiss may wake her, but nothing was now as it had been on the morning of her fifteenth birthday. It only seemed that way. So her father and mother woke up and behaved as if nothing had happened in the interim, and the marriage was duly arranged.

Things merely looked the same, but nothing was. The household was careful not to discuss their nightmares, and averted their eyes from windows which overlooked the surrounding countryside. The huge hedge was trimmed but not uprooted: it had its uses.

18

Human beings who have acquired a sense of history must lose their innocence. Etched in the memory, engraved on bone. It is true for the individual, and the human race.

History begins with the Book of Genesis. Repeatedly, with every birth. Those first days in the garden. Before stasis has become progression, change.

A newborn child has no history. Just sensation, changing light, warmth and cold. Pink roses climbing up the nursery wall, a door, a window, familiar voices. Steps lead into the garden, but what lies beyond? Find the gate, lift the latch, peer through the gaps in the picket fence. Curiosity is as natural as hunger or thirst.

History begins when yesterday is not quite like today. Today it is raining, yesterday it did not. History begins when last year's summer was hotter, sunnier. And when last year's sandals are too small. Time becomes linear, like a ship leaving a dying wake on receding water. And with it comes loss, a necessary exchange.

The history of the world, of earth-shaking events which will change the fate of nations, is subtly intertwined with the changing world of the growing child, only the child knows nothing of this. I hear the telephone ring beyond the nursery door, footsteps hurry down the corridor to answer it. Who is speaking? What is the message? I listen hard to my mother's voice, but pick up no inkling.

I am going to school. I have a brand-new satchel, with a slate, and a sponge in a little box to wipe it clean. Now I am not going to school. The satchel stays in the cupboard. I can write my name, but I still cannot read. I do not know why I am not going to school. I do not know how to ask the right questions. Or perhaps I do, but nobody is willing to give me the right answer. Nobody wants to play. My father is not coming home, my mother is always out, or on her way out, and does not bring me back a present. The servants whisper behind closed doors. Nobody talks to me, or organizes games. Or teaches me to read. Half the rooms are dark and deserted. I am in the dark.

The innocent do not know, if they ask a question, whether the answer is a lie, a deliberate distortion of the truth.

Where is daddy?

Away on business.

Why are all the windows in the street broken?

They are putting in new ones.

Why can't I go to school?

It is shut.

When the fence is high enough, the walls thick, and the questioner young enough, such censorship will work. Unease stays subliminal, inarticulate, coming and going like passing clouds. Nevertheless, the world is changing for ever, and cannot be saved.

19

Genesis is inevitably followed by an exodus, but not to a land flowing with milk and honey.

Every child must make the journey, never without difficulty. Some have it harder than others.

In the past a child was sent away from home to serve in a strange household, as pageboy, apprentice, scullery maid. Or further: the drummer boy marching into battle on foreign soil, the naval cadet under sail on distant oceans, the child bride sent away to forge a political alliance or conjoin estates. Children sold into slavery, sent up filthy chimneys, used in the sex trade. Or packed off to boarding school to turn the child into a man, the mother's boy into his father's image, the girl into her mother's, a suitable wife.

The rite of passage can be sudden or gradual. Defloration, the monthly bleed for girls, a bloody nose on Friday night for boys.

The modern extended childhood does not necessarily postpone the exodus from Eden. It simply takes different forms, just as painful. Parental discord, the shock of divorce. A father broken by unemployment, a mother by cancer. Domestic violence, abusive stepfathers, quarrels, a clash of wills, the parent who is no longer a parent, the child who will not go on being a child, or, on the other hand, refuses to grow up and take responsibility. Loud music late at night, secrets in the bedroom, a house grown too small for a family grown unwieldy, walls too thin, chaos in constricted spaces.

The final expulsion can be as dramatic as anything in the Old Testament. An offspring kicked out of the house, or opting to run away. Pregnancy, drug addiction, sleeping rough in the big city. Not necessarily. It might happen in a minor key. Everyone trying hard to behave well, ease the rupture, apply psychology. Refusing to be provoked. Nevertheless it must happen. Expulsion and disobedience, two sides of the same coin. Knowledge, however acquired, means exodus. The disgruntled adolescent grown tall enough to reach the apple, peer over the fence. Driven by appetite, by curiosity, for him the Garden of Eden is a con trick, a world of make-believe and childish things. He is not a child now. No. Moreover, his father is not, repeat, not God. Which is not easy to forgive.

There is, however, a fundamental difference between this gradual exodus, a natural progression from innocence to experience, which we call growing up, and a violent expulsion from childhood, sudden and premature, which leaves an indelible mark.

I imagine Eve, fully formed but still a child at heart, dreaming of Eden after the expulsion, gradually adapting to the harsh wilderness years, but forever homesick for the earthly Paradise she had lost, its colours glowing brighter with every passing year, the fruit on its branches sweeter, every footpath, each shady retreat etched in the memory. How she would walk the remembered glades in the night, conjure up flowers she had touched or picked, berries she had tasted, insects she had watched crawling on a leaf in their own private world, unaware of her presence.

I know how she felt.

My own childhood ended suddenly with an exodus, abrupt, inexplicable.

I thought I was inhabiting Eden. Life was a cycle between summer and winter. Snow in the city, a sandy garden in summer, with fruit trees, flowerbeds, window boxes.

I was as yet too young to think about growing up, ageing, or death. Apart from day turning to night, winter to summer, life was fixed. Each tree, every person had their place in the universe. Old people just were: that a grandmother, or the bony old chap who swung his scythe to cut the long grass might vanish had not occurred to me.

I did not have a clue about history, not yet. No notion that I was standing on a conveyor belt, not solid ground. Everything looked firmly rooted, the cherry tree, the apartment building, streets and railway stations. And everybody looked like everyone else, except for their clothes of course: the chauffeur wore a uniform, so did our housemaid, and the policeman who stood at the corner of the street. His helmet was a different shape from the cap my grandmother's driver wore. I had seen other uniforms on display in a shop window on the street leading to the park but, when I asked, my nursemaid would not tell me what they were for. I sensed a mystery but, for the moment, forgot it. Later, much later, I would remember gazing at the brown uniforms behind glass, the tall leather boots. It was the refusal to answer my innocent question that stuck in my memory. Grown-ups had an answer for everything. But at that moment silence hung in the air.

Later, much later, I would recollect that uneasy silence, and know its import. I would know, what I had not understood at the time, how carefully the adults who surrounded me had spun a web of lies to protect me from knowing the truth of the world into which I had been born. How often singsongs had been organized in the nursery, far from the rooms facing the street, so that childish songs would drown out the shouting coming from below. Not every eventuality, however, can be foreseen. Plate glass windows, spectacularly broken, can be put back. That I might stop and stare at a display of brown-shirt uniforms, asking for an explanation, had not occurred to her.

So I did not know about the conveyor belt of history, or that I had been born into an imminent catastrophe which was gathering momentum as I played in my sandpit, ate cherries fresh off the tree, or took a winter walk in the park. I did not know I was not as other children, though I learnt the same nursery rhymes, sang identical songs, had my hair cut in the same fashion, celebrated my first day at school with a leather satchel strapped to my back and was duly photographed with the ceremonial cone filled with sweets. I was part of a history of which I knew nothing.

Exodus, when it came, was sudden and inexplicable. It made no sort of sense to a child who could barely write her own name, could not read, whose schooling had been abruptly ended only months after her first day, for whom linear progression had stopped just when it was about to begin, and for whom the nursery had, to all intents and purposes, become an isolation ward, a germ-free zone where no rumours of the outside world, no sounds of marching, shouting, ugly songs, were allowed to penetrate.

Every passage from innocence to experience varies. No exodus from Eden is quite like any other. I know now, for example, that children only a few years older than myself, say nine rather than six, knew precisely what was going on, and had been preparing, mentally, for the eventuality of emigration for months and years. Whilst I was laboriously practising pothooks with a dip pen, English was being taught in other rooms, the text of *Macbeth* studied. Mine was a school for well-to-do assimilated families. Children whose parents had not abandoned Judaism might have some inkling, not only of what was happening, but why. I was six years old, still waiting for Father Christmas. I had no notion why he failed to arrive during the winter of 1938.

Think of the story of Genesis. Perhaps God was wrong, and forbidden fruit was always a bad idea. My mother treated the nursery as a safe place, where hygiene ruled. I remember her coming in with a white overall, freshly starched, on top of her ordinary clothes. All my life I have suffered from allergies, including eczema, severe enough to make me an invalid for years. So I subscribe to the theory that infants and toddlers must be exposed to a certain amount of dirt in order to develop a healthy immune system.

Should I also have been exposed to a deadlier form of filth, running in every gutter of the streets I then thought of as home?

I do not know. Physical immunity is not the same as mental and emotional development. It takes place at a pace which is still largely a mystery. Experts make informed guesses. Educationalists speak of windows of opportunity. By which they mean reading, writing, sums, or musical appreciation. It may involve learning how to cross the road safely. It is not part of any primary curriculum to teach young children how to survive a major catastrophe, earthquake or nuclear holocaust. History, too, is kept benign. Not until they are fourteen or thereabouts do they begin to be taught its hideous aspects.

20

For the human race loss of innocence comes with loss of faith in God the Father, all-seeing, whose wisdom is beyond question. Something similar happens to the trusting child on finding that a parent is not perfect, cannot control our particular universe. Is subject to vulnerability.

As a small child I idolized my father. Living with him was fun: he could sing, swing me up in the air, give me a ride on his shoulders, pretend to be a tiger at bedtime, drive a car, put up huge flapping sails and make the yacht swish through the water at a tilt so I shrieked with the excitement of it. He was the spirit of sunlight and laughter and I had never seen it overcast by so much as a passing cloud, or his confidence other than absolute.

So when I saw him for the first time, haggard from illness and his weeks in Dachau, I was less struck by the change in him than the huge living room without its familiar furniture. And the fact that my childish astonishment made him laugh helped to deceive me into thinking, if only for the moment, that my father was still the man I had always known, always cheerful, always sure of himself.

I was ready to listen to any yarn, any fairy tale he chose to spin. Not that he was lying. No, he was leaving things out. I asked questions about England, and London, and he would tell me that London was often so foggy nobody could see where they were going, and taxis drove right into railway stations instead of waiting outside, and I was puzzled. It did not sound like a particularly nice place to go, not like the mountains and lakes of Switzerland where we went for holidays. Then there was a growing sense of unease at so much disruption, toys and people who had to be left behind, the yacht, the weekend house with its garden, friends. But my father was so happy to be going to this foreign country, it did not occur to me to ask the question I should have asked. Why? I supposed it was some sort of adventure, the desire for fresh woods and pastures new. Like in a story book. I thought I could understand that, just about. My parents were so *adventurous*.

On the morning of our departure I saw through the pretence. Unsmiling and edgy, I had never seen him so nervous, so anxious to leave the empty apartment and get going. My sudden distress did not touch or soften him, merely made him cross. He spoke sharply. If I had known a world I did not then know, and had the appropriate vocabulary, I would have called his behaviour that of a fugitive. A man on the run for his life.

Was it at this moment of exodus that I realized, not only that everything was changing, but that my father too had altered? Perhaps. He was older, thinner, unsmiling and tense, not much hair left on his head, but his bearing too, his relationship to the rest of the world and those around him had also changed.

My father was no longer God. I had caught a glimpse of it in the fearful concrete building where the man in a brown shirt with the red armband and high leather boots had sat looking down on us from his wooden podium as he examined our papers, but we had emerged unscathed from it and walked away, out into the fresh air, not speaking, holding hands, and nothing of the sort had recurred. It was weird, it was scary, but it was over.

It was on disembarking from the cross-Channel ferry at Harwich, after staying with friends in Holland, dark sky overhead, dark water briefly glimpsed from the gangway, that I fully understood the dwindling status of my darling father. Not only was my father not God, he was humble, a petitioner, trying to ingratiate himself. Six years old, I felt embarrassed on his behalf as he spoke to two immigration officers in dark-blue uniforms, listening to him speak in English in answer to their brief questions.

You and your wife? asked one of them.

And two kiddies, he replied, in a voice that was too sprightly, trying too hard to be at ease, colloquial.

I watched the two men, unsmiling, wooden-faced under their peaked caps, and knew they were not amused, that he had completely failed to win them over. I might not know much about English, but I understood that he had got it wrong. Not 'kiddies', I thought, never say it. I felt humiliated on his behalf. Was this a nice country? Perhaps he had been wrong about that too.

Loss of innocence involves a change in our feelings towards our parents. Where at first we loved them because of their infinite power over us, over the known world, our emotions later become charged with the knowledge of their vulnerability, fallibility and powerlessness.

We begin by thinking that our parents are responsible for us. Sooner or later we realize, whether we like it or not, that our responsibility is to them.

21

How did Eve cope after the exodus from Eden? No doubt with difficulty. Quite apart from the pain of forcible expulsion from all she knew and loved, day to day existence was suddenly full of unforeseeable difficulties, deprivations, anxieties. She was a homeless refugee in a hostile environment, and the possibility of danger was ever present, hovering in the sky overhead, or lurking unseen in the alien wilderness. A consciousness of shame and nakedness did not help, and she undoubtedly went through bouts of depression, days when storms, cold weather or lack of food simply got too much for her, and Adam would return from the hunt to find her bitter and angry, seething with a resentment which, in the absence of God, had to be turned on the next best thing: him.

Adam did his best to be patient and understanding, but he himself coped far better with his changed circumstances. He quite enjoyed the excitement of the hunt, exploring new bits of territory, and scarcity of prey meant that he was often absent for several days at a stretch. On his return she would either weep or reproach him, and the sight of meat for their empty stomachs did not necessarily mollify her.

Adam, conscious of his position as head of the family, tried to soothe her, and put her moods down to the mysteries of her sex. She found it less easy to cope with their unhappy situation, the curse put upon them, the lack of creature comforts and, worst of all, the loneliness which exile from Eden had brought, a sense of isolation that nothing could still. After the boys were born their father impressed upon them from a very early age that it was their duty to look after their mother in his frequent absences. Life, he said, had not always been as it was now, and their mother had never got over the dramatic change of circumstances. So, he said sternly, no arguments, no pranks, no childish behaviour. There were, as we know, to be consequences.

22

This is how I remember it.

Feeling responsible for my mother. Trying so hard to take care of her. My father, absent for months, coming back briefly for a weekend leave in his army uniform, telling me to be good, look after my mother. Not to add to her difficulties. I did, I do, I protested, and I really did try. I dusted, swept, tried to pre-empt her wishes. I bought little gifts, not just on birthdays. It got too much for me, over six long years. The gifts were never big enough, quickly forgotten. The room I had swept had to be re-swept. I had to guard my tongue, always. If she made a parental decision which broke my heart (and she did) I had to keep my thoughts to myself, say nothing. I had been taught that it was her feelings which mattered, mine were irrelevant.

Needless to say, all this had its consequences.

Loss of innocence, of course.

But more, far more. I lost my mother, she her child. Try as we might, through all the long years of 'peace', we never succeeded in finding each other again. Just an occasional armistice.

23

Eve had to eat of the fruit of the Tree of Knowledge. Why else was it there? And one day, after a lifetime in the wilderness, she would understand that the home from which she had been expelled had never been the idyll she remembered with such longing. The Serpent had always been there, lurking in the undergrowth, only the newborn eyes of innocence had made her blind, dazzled as she was by the natural splendour of sun and moon, the infinite variety of colour and shape, leaf and flower, bird and insect.

Sooner or later we must all eat of the fruit, and its taste is bitter.

Sooner or later every one of us must learn that there is no going back, that the garden of childhood was just an illusion.

But it will not let go of us, that is the irony. It gleams at the end of a long dark tunnel, bright as ever. At the end of the journey, every hope, every illusion shattered, weary of body and mind, it is only there we want to go.

Those who live to grow old eventually die of homesickness. Hear them, in their final hours, crying out for a long dead relative, babbling of green fields and summer picnics, speaking a mother tongue suppressed during a lifetime of exile.

Everything else is forgotten. The long dark journey through the wilderness, the bitter taste left in the mouth by the fruit of the Tree, rage, hatred, a sense of injustice that nothing can appease, the contamination of evil that hangs in the air despite years of wind and rain, melting snows and changing seasons. The ash of murdered innocence falls from the sky, however bright the sun. It catches in the throat, makes the eyes water helplessly.

But, when the end comes, home is still home. Where else can the soul go?

24

How to live with it, this dualism?

All my life I have wrestled with it, the fact that the best of times were so fatally flawed, that everything I cherished would be forfeited, was inevitably lost even before it had begun, that the golden sands of time were running out whilst I was playing with it in the garden, raking the footpaths, filling my bucket in the sandpit, or drawing architectural plans for future homes with the heel of my shoe in its malleable surface.

All my life I have tried to fit the pieces together, dark and light, known and unknown, horror and happiness.

Is there, can there ever be, a coming together? I do not know. Was Blake, when he wrote his poems, infused with the spirit of irony? I do not think so. Everything about them, about him, sends a very different message. A marriage between heaven and hell. Dark and light, night of the soul and sunrise. Seeing the world in a grain of sand, as I did, each a precious jewel with a different colour. Finding the worm in the heart of the rose.

All my life, from the age of thirteen, I have told myself that cruelty has a human face, terror the human form. This is a knowledge I cannot escape. But I remember how it was to see the human form divine imbued with a glow of peace and love. Its arms cradled me, its face bent over my pillow, its hands soothed my every ache and pain.

It matters, to hold on to the vision, despite knowledge of the contradiction. To cherish innocence, the fleeting moment. To foster the child within is to foster joy. In the absence of faith, there is nothing else.

FOUR

I

And what of the demons, the hideous creatures lurking in the shadows of the forest through which I must travel to get back to my starting point? Still hungry for blood, they wait for me. They have been waiting for me for a very long time, knowing I must pass this way eventually, however long the procrastination. Sooner or later I would, heart beating too fast, dread in every footstep, warily tread the path through the trees, afraid to look in the undergrowth for fear of what I might find, catch a glimpse of, but also knowing that failure to do so was worse, a haunted imagination is so much more terrifying, infinitely fecund, summoning up monstrous images endlessly changing shape, a ghostly parade of horror, dwindling, receding into the mist, only to re-emerge more lifelike and frightening than during its last apparition. So it is better to look, eyes wide open, jaw tight, to left and right, peering behind every tree, examining the undergrowth for signs: footprints, bones, remnants of human hair.

In the end I had to set out, there being nowhere else to go. Confront my demons, heart beating too fast, dread in every footstep. Afraid of what I might find, or worse still, fail to find.

Going back is so much harder. This time we know what

lurks, how the story ended. I am not the little girl who skipped so happily through the trees, diverted by pretty things, nature's trinkets. Speaking politely to strangers, regardless of their clothing. I see her, weightless, light as thistledown, running through the trees, holding her grandmother's hand, joyous in the morning air, blue sky glimpsed through the topmost branches of trees.

Where, if anywhere, is she to be found? I sense she is shadowing me, playing hide-and-seek through the trees. I feel as though, at any moment, she will creep up behind me and take hold of my hand.

2

But the hand that is holding mine belongs to another, my granddaughter. Young, truly innocent, on the threshold. Time has come full circle, and everything seems like an afterimage, an echo of what was. Only now I am the end, and she is the beginning. Nevertheless we hold hands: I feel her, she feels me. We speak to each other, as grown-ups never do. I tell her things. With her, through her clear eyes, I see the world afresh. I bend to her eye level, measure my steps to her short legs as she goes with a hop and a skip alongside. I speak to her as she is now, and to what she will become in the future, knowing, as I do, that she will remember, not everything, but moments, gleams of gold in the dross, cleansed with the years, the ever-running river of time as night falls.

I remember. Her being here, holding my hand, reminds me, with an immediacy that is bittersweet.

And so there are shadows following us. I sense her, my grandmother, hovering at my shoulder, her footfalls stepping lightly wherever I go, her hand holding mine, is it, or is it I who am now her? I think I am imbued with her spirit, comprehending how she felt as she saw me coming through the school gate and walked, holding my hand in hers, down the tree-lined avenue or, walking through the wood, taught me how to turn a dry autumn leaf into a miraculous cobweb with an ordinary clothes brush after we took it home.

It feels like a resurrection, this ghost hovering like my shadow in the sunlight. I am her, but I am also the child I am taking to the park, to the playground, the zoo.

There is sunlight, there is shadow. At this moment there is scarcely a cloud in the sky, the world shimmers, glows with colour, still the old world, but for the moment it seems new.

3

I am old now, as he was, as she was, on the day of their death. The unknown day, into the mouth of hell, their beloved faces merging with the millions, the unrecorded millions and their children going into the dark. I have retraced their last steps as far as I could, fearful with their fear, their terror of the unknown, appalled by the infinity of suffering, humiliation. I have picked up the odd clue too: I know that my grandfather kept his pride to the last, and this recognition made me proud for him, and of him. Not much, I know, in the ordinary way of things, but theirs was no ordinary path. After following their footsteps, heart beating too fast, fearful of shadows lurking in the trees, I had found a sign, a signal, lying on the path. It had been lying there for fifty years, waiting for me to find it. I only had to look, keep looking, to get the message left behind for whoever cared enough to search. Not closure, no, but a touching of the two ends of the circle. I saw him now, as I had long ago seen him at the window of the airport. Now, as then, I could see him wholly for a moment, even if I was invisible to him.

I am old now, as he was, as she was, and though I can have no truthful inkling of what it is like to end their lives as they did, I do know what it is like to reach their age.

Death is less terrifying when so much has been taken away, not knowing the end is the only terror. I also know, as I could not when I was a child, though I might have sensed it, how much my very existence meant to them. I understand this simply because I too am a grandmother now. This is why, every time I take her small hand in mine, I am conscious of undying love. It grows stronger as I do with her what she, he, did with the child that was me, that is still me.

In my end is my beginning. I have come through the forest, faced its terrors, real and imaginary, and reached the fringe, where sunlight glows on the meadow. I want to put it behind me, go back to my starting point, as children do in fairy tales. Unscathed, obviously not. My life is not a fairy tale, and the child who escapes the forest cannot possibly be the unknowing child who was sent into it.

But perhaps the beloved dead do watch over us, as they so often do in Grimms' stories. If only because early loss will never dwindle into forgetfulness. Those taken from us too soon refuse to die, go with us, wherever we go.

4

Walking in the spring sunshine, under the budding trees, I hold her small hand in mine. Now and then I squeeze it, and she squeezes mine in return. It is a little game we play. Her skinny little legs hop and skip to keep up with me. Chattering happily, her trust in me is absolute. Rightly. I would die to keep her safe. If I had to die far off, in hell, I would find comfort in knowing no harm could come to her. Far off, in another country. I would hold on to that, almost to the last, perhaps beyond. It would help me to face any hardship, I think.

I hope so.

They walk with me. I am the child who walks between them.

We stand on a bridge spanning the small lake. My granddaughter peers over the rail at our reflection and laughs.

I can see you, she says.

I see you too, I answer.

A NOTE ON THE TYPE

The text of this book is set in Fournier. Fournier
is derived from the *romain du roi*, which was created
towards the end of the seventeenth century for
the exclusive use of the Imprimerie Royale from
designs made by a committee of the Académie of
Sciences. The original Fournier types were cut
by the famous Paris founder Pierre Simon Fournier
in about 1742. These types were some of the
most influential designs of the eighteenth century,
and are counted among the earliest examples of the
'transitional' style of typeface. This Monotype
version dates from 1924. Fournier is a light, clear
face whose distinctive features are capital letters that
are quite tall and bold in relation to the lower-case
letters, and *decorative italics, which show the influence
of the calligraphy of Fournier's time.*